Pencil portrait of Eric Cordingly *by POW HC Gordon, Changi October 1942*

Down to Bedrock

The Diary and Secret Notes of a
Far East Prisoner of War Chaplain 1942-45

Eric Cordingly

Edited by **Louise Cordingly**

Front Cover: pen and ink drawing of a funeral procession in Changi by POW Payne.

Design by MADE Agency Ltd
Typesetting in 11pt Bell MT
Printed in England by Swallowtail Print, Norwich, Norfolk

Published by Art Angels Publishing Ltd, Norwich

ISBN – 978 0 9926954 0 8

CONTENTS

PREFACE
by Louise Cordingly

"The most wonderful time in my life, in spite of the grim and hungry times [...] For once, and for three and a half years, the thin veneer of civilization, or reticence, had been stripped from men. We were all down to bedrock. One saw people as they really were."

My father wrote these words from his Rectory in Norfolk more than twenty years after he was released from captivity. Like many former prisoners of war, Eric Cordingly rarely talked of his wartime experiences. Perhaps he wanted to spare his family from hearing the full horror of his three and a half years in captivity in the Far East. But we always knew how important that period was to him. He kept his wartime papers and took them with him as we moved across England for the Church. In 1967 he drew on these papers to write a reflection for a collection of prisoners' experiences, published as *Beyond Hatred*.

After his death in 1976, my mother Mary, took his wartime papers into safe-keeping. For years Eric's collection lay guarded but uninspected. After Mary died in 2011, our family felt that the time was finally right to look at Eric's papers. We opened folders which had not been touched in decades. It was a breathtaking discovery. We found a collection of diaries, notes, sketches, maps, cards, letters, orders of service, and a burial register. We even found an entire typed manuscript called *Captive Christians*, complete with foreword and dedication.

In these folders, Eric's wartime story lay preserved but in pieces. My three brothers and I have decided to reconstruct those years on his behalf, confident that he would want future generations of his family to learn the truth of his experiences as a prisoner of war. He described his three and a half years as a prisoner of war as the most meaningful of his life. We hope that these, his wartime papers, will explain why.

Eric Cordingly in World War II

"I think I always felt a bit in the way in the army," reflected Eric Cordingly on his first two years as a military chaplain before he became a prisoner of war, "officers and men were always very kind to a chaplain and did all they could to help him get on with his job, but one often seemed to be in the way."

During this early stage of the war, there appeared to be little military need for an unarmed, transplanted rector from the Cotswolds. Eric Cordingly was assigned to a territorial battalion of the Royal Northumberland Fusiliers which soon found itself retreating from the German army on the beaches at Dunkirk.

"The hours spent there were among the most unpleasant that I can remember," he later recalled.

In October 1941, Cordingly's battalion was despatched abroad and for months, the soldiers sailed East. Britain was about to face a new enemy : the Japanese Empire. Following its assault on Pearl Harbor on 7th December 1941, Japan moved quickly to conquer Britain's colonial territories in the Far East. The Imperial Japanese Army announced that it planned to liberate its fellow Asian peoples from weak-spirited Westerners.

"When you encounter the enemy after landing, regard yourself as an avenger come at last face to face with his father's murderer," an anti-West manual instructed Japanese soldiers.

Eric Cordingly arrived with the 18th Division days before Singapore's final stand. It was to be a short battle. Japanese forces invaded the island and broke into Alexandra Hospital in Singapore, killing doctors, nurses, a chaplain, and more than 200 hundred patients in their beds. On 15th February 1942, Britain's commanding general surrendered to Japan. Winston Churchill declared the fall of Singapore the worst disaster and largest capitulation in British history.

The Imperial Japanese Army suddenly found itself with more than 50,000 British and Australian prisoners of war. It had a low regard for its captives; surrender was seen as moral failure. Japan decided to hold its POWs in an expansive, former Allied barracks in Changi, in the north-east of Singapore. The Changi prisoner of war camp became the largest grouping of Allied captives in the new Japanese Empire.

"For us the war was over," Eric Cordingly wrote after the war, "We were all stunned and it took some time to get our bearings. None of us knew what the future would hold, and it was now that a chaplain had the most wonderful opportunity."

Cordingly began by converting an abandoned mosque into a church which he named St George's. He encouraged his fellow prisoners to make use of this church and was heartened when they did so. The 30-year-old chaplain finally had a worthwhile role in an army which was no longer able to fight.

His experiences inspired him to type a 150 page manuscript while he was still in the camp. He documented with satisfaction congregation numbers and church activities.

"I wonder as we all do, how long this captivity will last, will it be months or years? " he wrote, "How will it all end, and how shall we be released?"

Cordingly even drew up plans to publish his manuscript as a book. This manuscript, titled *Captive Christians*, is now reproduced in its entirety in this book.

In this, his first period of captivity in Singapore, Cordingly rarely allowed his recorded thoughts to drift to his family. His wife Mary was left in Leckhampton Rectory in Gloucestershire with their two young sons David, 3, and John, 1.

"In spite of personal loneliness I am convinced that all is well with my home and my wife and two sons," he wrote in *Captive Christians*, "One develops a terrific faith in these things."

This faith was to help him survive the next, most harrowing period of his time as a prisoner of war : a year on the Burma Railway.

By May 1942, Japan's new Empire stretched 3000 miles from Tokyo to Burma. It needed to secure the supply lines to the furthest reaches of its new conquests. The Allies continued to attack Japanese shipping in the Indian Ocean. So Japan decided to consider overland routes instead. In particular it set its sights on one plan - the construction of a railway from Thailand to Burma. In 1885 British engineers had considered and rejected the same idea. Building a railway through mountains and thick jungle would be too difficult, too expensive, and would cost too many lives.

But the Japanese Empire of 1942 believed that it had a perfect source of cheap, dispensable labour : its 50,000 Allied prisoners of war in Singapore. Their deaths, and those of many more native workers, would not matter. So, Japan set itself a target : the construction of 258 miles of railway in just 18 months.

In April 1943, Eric Cordingly was sent with 7000 fellow prisoners from Singapore to Thailand as part of 'F' Force. The Japanese authorities initially told the prisoners that they were being sent to Thailand in order to recover their strength. The men were told to expect blankets and even gramophones. But these were false promises. Upon arrival, the captives' real task became clear.

"I have pleasure to lead you on the charge of the last stretch of Railway Construction Wardoom," proclaimed Colonel Sijuo Nakamura, the Japanese Commander of POW Camps in Thailand, "Those who fail to reach objective in charge by lack of health or spirit is considered in the Japanese Army most shameful deed. Devotion to Death is good."

Over the next 12 months, 'F' Force was to suffer some of the most devastating losses of any group forced to work on the Burma Railway. One official report documents that within the first four months, 90% of this Force was sick. In the end, 45% of the men in 'F' Force died while working on the Burma railway.

Cordingly spent most of this year in and around Kanburi (Kanchanaburi), Thailand, close to where the railway was being built. In Kanburi, he tried to recreate a version of the church he'd built up in Changi, Singapore. He took with him a brass cross a fellow prisoner had made for him in Changi and created a makeshift St George's Church in a corner of the new POW camp. He also kept pencil notes using whatever materials he could find - a children's exercise book, blue airmail paper, and isolated scraps of paper. They are the thoughts of a man who does not know whether or not he will survive. Those notes, combined with his short military report, are reproduced in this book as *Living Skeletons*. Cordingly found that a chaplain, so useless in combat, was now indispensable.

"Men were stunned and apathetic, but slowly the spiritual side revived and flourished as never before," he wrote, "Men had been so near death – life for them had been stripped of its veneer, stark reality had faced them, they expected to be met on those terms. They talked about death and many is the time at the bedside of a dying man he has asked me to pray for his death, for his peace, for release from his abject misery."

By the end of 1943, the main work on the Burma railway had been completed. Cordingly volunteered to stay on to minister to patients in a field hospital. In April 1944, he was sent back down to Changi, Singapore. He and his fellow prisoners were held in crowded conditions next to and inside Changi prison.

"We were to spend another seventeen months under the shadow of the gaol walls in Changi," he wrote after the war, "These were grim months in many ways and our rations were at starvation level."

The prisoners set about rebuilding the ordered life of their first period in Changi. Cordingly constructed two new versions of St George's Church. Other captives started up university courses, societies, factories, and workshops. Prisoners worked as carpenters, blacksmiths, watchmakers, and even carried out typewriter repairs. A working party of 900 men was used to flatten an area near the camp and turn it into a Japanese military airbase. Others were sent to work on the docks.

In November 1944, prisoners at Changi saw American B29 bombers flying overhead. For them, this was a first sign of the war's changing tide. In the next few months, Allied air raids against Japanese forces continued. Prisoners at Changi were able to follow the news on secret radios. The shift in the war brought its own anxieties. Inside the camp there was a real fear that the Japanese might decide to kill their prisoners before accepting surrender.

No extensive notes survive from this, Eric Cordingly's final period of imprisonment. But his collection of papers, reproduced here as *Under the Shadow of the Gaol Walls*, include a number of Christmas cards that he received in December 1944. 'May 1945 see you on the lawns of Leckhampton' one prisoner wrote to him.

On 6th and 9th August 1945, the US dropped atomic bombs on Hiroshima and Nagasaki. A week later, on 15th August, Emperor Hirohito broadcast the announcement of Japan's surrender. Their guards at first refused to admit the Japanese defeat. But, soon, paratroopers entered the camp. Eric Cordingly's three and a half years as a prisoner of war were at an end.

LC

Eric Cordingly Timeline : 1939 - 45

September 1939
Rector in Gloucestershire ; appointed air raid warden.

March 1941
Appointed Chaplain with Territorial Battalion of Royal Northumberland Fusiliers ; deployed to France.

May 1941
Evacuated from Dunkirk.

October 1941
Deployed to Far East with 18th Division.

February 1942
Captured in fall of Singapore ; held in Changi prisoner of war camp.

April 1943
Sent to work on construction of the Burma Railway in Thailand.

April 1944
Sent back to Singapore ; held at Changi prison.

September 1945
Leaves Changi prison after Japanese surrender.

October 1945
Returns home to Gloucestershire.

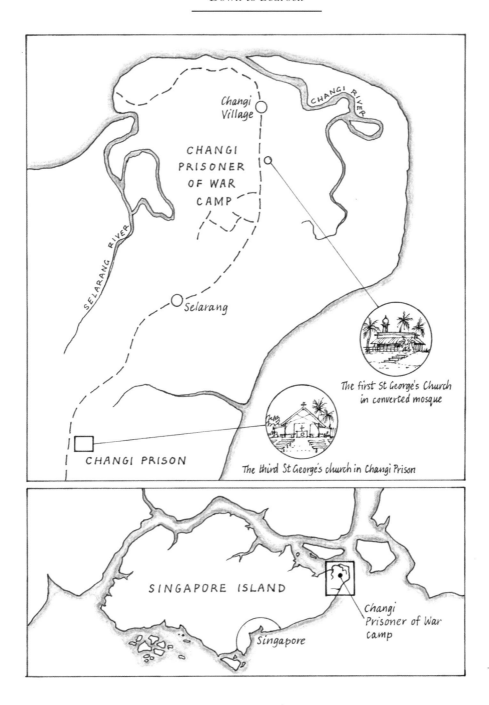

Maps to show the location of Changi prisoner of war camp, Changi Prison and
St George's Mark 1 and Mark 111. *Drawn by David Cordingly*

Captive Christians
February 1942 - April 1943
Changi POW Camp, Singapore
Eric Cordingly's manuscript

Cover design by fellow POW for Eric's proposed book *Captive Christians*, which neatly combines both the cross and the onion dome of the converted mosque.

FOREWORD

It is with the greatest pleasure that I write a foreword to this book. Lieut. General Percival, C.B., C.B.E., D.S.O., M.C., G.O.C., Malaya Command, in an address to all Chaplains in the Changi P.O.W. Camp, said "You have had your great opportunity in this Camp and you have seized it with both hands". This record is the story of one such opportunity – a record as magnificent as it is unique and one of which the author may be justly proud.

As acting A.C.G. Far East from the time of the fall of Singapore in February 1942, until Mr Cordingly was transferred to another up-country P.O.W. Camp in April 1943, I was in the closest touch with him and his work at St George's. Of the 17 churches which we were able to establish, equip and operate, I regarded St George's as the "Cathedral Church" (so to speak) of the area. Its beauty of architecture and design and the dignity of its setting and its services, together with the faithful ministry of word and sacrament, combined to attract enormous numbers of men to all its services. It was always an inspiration to be present and preach when I had the opportunity.

Mr Cordingly did a job of work in St. George's which is bound to have very far reaching effects on the Church of the future, and many men will return to their own country after this time of captivity with a new idea of God and religion as a consequence. Such is his reward. He would ask for no other.

J.N. Lewis Bryan, A/Asst. Chap. General, Far East. April, 1943

For a life of fellowship shared
In captivity with the Officers
And men, Gunners, Sappers, R.A.O.C.[*],
And R.A.S.C.[+] of the 18th Division,
and for the privilege of serving
in battle in France and the Far
East with the Officers and men
of the 9th Bn, The Royal
Northumberland Fusiliers, these
words are DEDICATED with humble gratitude

* Royal Army Ordnance Corps
+ Royal Army Service Corps

The day thou gavest, Lord is ended,
The darkness falls at Thy behest;
To Thee our morning hymns ascended,
Thy praise shall sanctify our rest

We thank thee that Thy church, unsleeping,
While earth rolls onward into light,
Through all the world her watch is keeping,
And rests not now by day or night

As o'er each continent and island
The dawn leads on another day,
The voice of prayer is never silent,
Nor dies the strain of praise away

The sun that bids us rest is waking
Our brethren 'neath the western sky,
And hour by hour fresh lips are making
Thy wondrous doings heard on high.

So be it, Lord; Thy throne shall never,
Like earth's proud empires, pass away;
Thy kingdom stands, and grows forever,
Till all Thy creatures own Thy sway

This became the prisoners' special hymn and was sung every Sunday in captivity
and has been used at POW memorial services ever since.

INTRODUCTION
FOREWORD

As the days have passed in this life behind the
wire, it has seemed that perhaps the experiences of
prisoners herded together on a famous island so near the
equator have been unique. Perhaps so different from that
of popular imagination.   Then weeks drifted into months
and still life has been lived in a way that to many seems
almost miraculous.   Life that has for so many centred
round a little Church.   It is that life, those unique
and amazing happenings that it is a privilege to record.
It has been a day-to-day experience, and one that has
influenced some hundreds, no, it must be some thousands
of lives.

Grimness and greatness in wartime has been
rightly recorded, but that is not the purpose of these
pages, but rather the strange and really rather wonderful
life of a prisoner of war.   In the years that are ahead
there will be many whose faith means much, and who owe
the finding of that faith and its firm foundations to that
one-time mosque dwarfed by those tall clusters of

First page of diary typed by Eric when he was held captive in Changi POW Camp
from Feb 42 – April 43

INTRODUCTION

As the days have passed in this life behind the wire, it has seemed that perhaps the experiences of prisoners herded together on a famous island so near the equator have been unique. Perhaps so different from that of popular imagination. Then weeks drifted into months and still life has been lived in a way that to many seems almost miraculous. Life that has for so many centred round a little Church. It is that life, those unique and amazing happenings that it is a privilege to record. It has been a day-to-day experience, and one that has influenced some hundreds, no, it must be some thousands of lives.

Grimness and greatness in wartime has been rightly recorded, but that is not the purpose of these pages, but rather the strange and really rather wonderful life of a prisoner of war. In the years that are ahead there will be many whose faith means much, and who owe the finding of that faith and its firm foundations to that one-time mosque dwarfed by those tall clusters of cocoanut trees in that Far Eastern fortress of Singapore.

The glimpses of that life lived were written in captivity, their scrappiness is obvious, their lack of style is immediately apparent, but perhaps their reading will not be uninteresting. To the writer the life was one of thrilling inspiration, and it is in the hope that the reader may catch some glimpse of this amazing experience that these pages have been added to the already enormous lists of published efforts of amateur writers.

To those readers who shared that captivity, the writer apologises for the inadequacy of that which follows and to them he offers his gratitude and humble thanks, for they were in those days "Captive Christians".

COMMUNIQUE

The Japanese High Command has issued the following instructions:—

(i) The existing administrative and economic systems continue to exist, all personnel retaining their present positions for the time being.

(ii) Public utility services should be restored as quickly as possible, and all employees should continue in their normal duties for the time being.

(iii) Wireless communication and broadcasting is prohibited.

(iv) The air defence regulations are to be strictly enforced, with special reference to the control of lighting during the hours of darkness. The "brown out" and "black out" will therefore continue.

(v) No communication with the outside world is permitted.

(xi) No person may leave Singapore island without permission of the Japanese High Command.

(vii) All institutions and services relating to the public health and the care of the sick must be carefully supervised and any deficiencies made good as quickly as is practicable. The staff should carry on with their normal duties, tending the sick and wounded and prisoners.

(viii) The Japanese Army will afford protection to the civilian population. Civilians should remain in their normal places of residence, unless they have received special permission from the Japanese Army to move.

(ix) There is to be no spying or espionage against the Japanese.

2. The Civil Government is assisting in the restoration of normal conditions in Singapore. Committees will be set up to deal with (a) questions of administration, (b) public health, (c) economics and finance, (d) prisoners of war, (e) military affairs including the public peace, communications, war material and supplies, (f) naval affairs, (g) air affairs. There will also be a Liaison Committee, one of whose duties will be to arrange for the eventual transfer of administration to the Japanese High Command.

3. It is the duty of every man and woman in Singapore to co-operate in the task of restoring order and cleanliness in the town. We owe this to the wounded, for whom the existing facilities are inadequate; we must not allow the appearance of disease to reduce these facilities. We owe it also to all the women and children in the town, to all those who have been bereaved, or have lost all they possess. I am confident that everyone will help.

4. I thank all those who have rendered such devoted service during the past days. I thank the civil population for the way in which they have remained quiet.

T. S. W. THOMAS.

Feb. 16, 1942.

List of rules and prohibitions for POWs issued by Japanese High
Command on Feb 16th 1942, the day following their surrender.

It had been a nine days' wonder and while it lasted tense and exciting, but in reality rather more tragic and shattering. There was greatness in sacrifice and service, but war waged with modern weapons can have no glamour. It all ended on that Sunday, 15th February, 1942 at four o'clock in the afternoon. The cease fire order had been given, the siege of Singapore had finished. For us this had been preceded by months of travel; Canada, the West Indies, South and East Africa and India had all been visited, and our arrival on the island of Singapore coincided with the barrage of the Jap guns from the mainland of Malaya, across that half-mile strip of water. Bombed on the last stage of our voyage at sea, we were to land on an island that was devoid of air and sea power, onto what we imagined was an impregnable fortress.

This was an island fortress if attacked from the sea, but evidently attack from the mainland was not expected. The half of the island that was overshadowed by land and separated from it by a narrow ribbon of water, was without a pill-box. Not a strand of wire defended the shore. It must have been assumed that if attack was to be made, it would come from the South, from the sea.

I am attempting to assume a role which I am quite unfitted to fulfil, and to speak of matters that are no concern of mine. That tale is not mine.

We were stunned to hear that we were to lay down our arms. I had wondered from time to time as the battle became fiercer, it seemed that this action would end in massacre or surrender. We were fighting in an area perhaps five miles wide and two miles deep, we were in the outskirts of Singapore, behind us was the town with its population of nearly a million. The Japs were free to plaster us with shells, and mortars and dive bombing and pattern bombing. The reservoirs and ammunition dumps were in enemy hands.

I had spent these last days in our advanced medical post, helping the doctor with the casualties which were brought in in their dozens all day. The shrapnel from mortar shells had torn great ugly wounds, one almost longed for the clean cut of small arms fire. All this came to an end at four o'clock on that Sunday. We were tired, it had meant just snatches of sleep for ten days, and I suppose the relief was terrific, but there was that feeling that this ought not to be, we should not have been forced to lay down our arms, but the decision was not ours, and we presume it had been taken after a review of the general position.

Knowing the number of the casualties which had poured into the R.A.P.,[*] and the nature of the wounds, I realised that there must be many of our dead lying in the Jap lines. I tackled Divisional H.Q. and asked for permission to go and bury them. I set off in an ambulance with six stretcher bearers and our M.O.,[†] and as we were wearing the Red Cross armbands, getting past the Jap sentries was easy. Wiry little fellows are the Japs, not well dressed or equipped, and very small in stature compared with ourselves. No objection was raised to the ambulance and going along Mount Pleasant Road (which is part of the very best residential area of Singapore) we came across our dead – a body here and there – on the side of the road – in the ditches – and we stopped and gave each a Christian burial, using as graves the many slit trenches which were to be found everywhere. One service was said over a grave of nine officers and men of the 4th Suffolks, who had just been buried by men of the Regiment. The following morning I set out again, this time going several miles into enemy lines, and up the Kheam Hoch Road, where I had heard there had been an ambush. Here we came to the most awful carnage I have yet seen. On a bend in the road were two burnt out Bren Carriers, with four or five bodies sprawled across the road – bodies quite naked. Leaning from the Carriers were more – parts of men- burnt stumps of men – and this after two days of tropical sun – the stench of this scene will be with me always. Along in the ditches were others – fifty or more – an officer spread-eagled in the middle of the road – quite unrecognisable. I went from body to body trying to remove Identity Discs and personal effects. It was impossible to tell whether they were English, Jap or Indian – swollen, sizzling, bursting corpses. We buried each one – some who could not be moved we covered with earth. Others we buried in a large bomb crater.

The Japs were courteous and kind, and led me into houses and behind thick undergrowth where there were more dead. Not once did I receive anything but kindness from our victors, even to the offering of cigarettes, and to standing around the graveside for the short committal service. Perhaps just one incident marred their behaviour. In the morning a Nippon soldier took me through a native village past some Jap tanks (which I suppose were responsible for the chaos and death on the road) into a garden. There he pointed to a mat, which I raised and saw five Indian soldiers dead, shot through the chest and head, but with their hands tied together. When I came back later in the day to bury them, they had been buried by the Japs, perhaps there was some reason for this.

* Regimental Aid Post
† Medical Officer

Detailed instructions issued by the British Army in Malaya for the identification and burial of their dead, especially designed for the local conditions. "A rough sketch relative to some co-ordinate should be made to assist in tracing graves after the grass and jungle have grown over them"

Page from Eric's 'Burial Returns' book. For several days after the capitulation, he went out in an ambulance with 6 stretcher bearers to find and bury the dead. On 18th February 1942 he recorded "5 Indians buried by Japanese in village behind houses (N. side). The Indians had been shot with hands tied behind backs"

I can say with perfect honesty that this day was the worst I have ever lived through. Fighting in the tropics is a terrible thing – the aftermath is worse.

With the help of the ambulance and my armband I was able to get about and do what I could for our stranded troops, who were compelled to remain by the side of the road in groups. Food and drink for them was a necessity. For two days I was able to drive around either on my own or with another officer.

Three days after that order to cease fire, the road which runs from the town of Singapore to the North-East corner of the island was packed with troops marching to captivity in good order and good spirits. These ranks of khaki clad, battle stained men plodded through the heat to that part of the island that was to serve as a prison camp to this surrendered force. Ambulances filled with the wounded threaded their way through this dusty, sweating mass. Between the thirteenth and fifteenth milestones on this ribbon-like road was a vast military barracks, in part dimmed by camouflage, and battered by bombing and shelling.

Into this area throughout the evening and night of Ash Wednesday fagged men trooped. It was for them the end of the battle of Malaya, and the nine day siege of Singapore.

With my Battalion 9 R.N.F. I found that we have been allotted an area with the Divisional Troops, which were made up of the Sappers, and the R.A.S.C. and the R.A.O.C. I have had real cause for happiness that I should be living amongst such a fine crowd of officers and men.

Eric's Identity disc engraved in English and Japanese.

FEBRUARY 1942

POW sketch of a Japanese guard at Changi POW Camp.

The whole area is quite free of Jap guards, very occasionally a Jap patrol of 3 (known to us as Freeman, Hardy and Willis) will ride through on bicycles, or officers will rush through in cars. We are quite free to roam about our area as we wish. The first few days here were spent in settling in, some in buildings, some in tents, others in all sorts of weird and fantastic home-made huts and shelters. In the area in which we live there are about 3500 of us. Officers and men are together, which is most unusual in prison camps. The situation is even more unique and odd, because we are living, as it were, in a peace-time camp, with the officers looking after the men. We organise our own routine, and punishments, and fatigues, and rules, and at present have provided our own guards. There are no Jap guards, and we have now wired ourselves in, and have our own military police at the various gates. Of course there are Japanese in evidence outside, and they have warned us that anyone seen outside the wire will be shot; three Gunners and six Australians have already been executed. It would seem that the Nippon army has a high respect for this surrendered force. In wandering freely over our area, I have seldom come across a Jap, of course as I have mentioned there are rules and regulations. We are surrounded on three sides by sea, and escape might seem to be easy, but the Japs know the impossibility, they are patrolling the narrow straits between us and the mainland of Malaya. The many islands around us are Jap controlled. At the present all the land south of Singapore is in Jap hands, and the nearest British possession is India, and that is 1500 miles off, these gloomy prospects coupled with a tropical climate and all that it means presents an enormous obstacle. During our first few weeks we were allowed to walk along to the beaches and enjoy marvellous bathing, but we presume that since the Jap Navy has moved into the Naval base, that privilege has been withdrawn.

For the first week we lived on the rations we had brought with us, and this meant six army biscuits a day with perhaps a sardine for breakfast and some "bully" beef stew at 6.30 in the evening, this food made up our two main meals a day, though at midday we had two of the six biscuits with some pale, unsweetened, milkless tea. By drinking our tea this way we were able to drink it three times a day. It is wet and warm and very refreshing, but it is not tea nor is it very palatable. It has been the case of tightening the belt, and ignoring the pangs of hunger. A big thrill in a day would be the sharing of a cocoanut, which had found its way into somebody's hands. We are surrounded by palm trees and there are loads of cocoanuts, but these are being collected by our authorities and issued with the rations.

Now in our third week here the supply of biscuits and other oddments is exhausted so that we are dependent on the rations supplied by our captors. In consequence we are being fed on what is supposed to be the Japanese field army scale of rations, which is the scale for the ordinary Jap soldier. It should be as follows: Meat 1 ¾ ozs, Flour 1 ¾ ozs, Sugar 7/10 of oz, Tea 1/6 of oz, salt 1/6 of oz, vegetables 3 ½ oz., and rice 17 ozs. In actual fact we don't necessarily receive these rations, our rice ration has never been more than 12 oz, and as yet our vegetable supply is almost nil. These are our daily supplies. I would defy any European to eat 17 ounces of rice in a day, especially if it has to be eaten as rice or very lightly flavoured with oddments. The most we have managed to eat in a day is ten to twelve ounces, and this rests very heavily in the "tummy", though in the times ahead rice was eaten in larger quantities.

So far our meals have been fairly good, and except for an occasional "off" day, they have been quite appetising due to the ingenuity of our mess cooks. Curry, rice fish cakes, rice and "bully" beef stew, rice and cheese. In the days ahead we hope for inspiration from our cooks for rice is not our food, and one misses bread, fats and butter and vegetables and meat. Still there is no longer that completely empty feeling, rice makes a fairly adequate lining, though this "fullness" wears off in about an hour, and thought about food must be put aside, or one becomes quite desperate.

FROM MOSQUE TO CHURCH

It must be obvious that in our present circumstances as prisoners of war the work of a padre can be tremendous, his scope is as never before in his life, his opportunities are enormous. Together men have faced grim things and are ready to turn to God. Men now have leisure forced upon them. Gone temporarily is the rush and hurry and noise of a working, fighting world and away in a quiet corner of the world men are inevitably taking stock of themselves. As a padre one is so grateful for the chance one has been given, and the response to his efforts is repaid all the way along.

On the day after our imprisonment, I discovered next to our billet a delightful building almost hidden by flowering shrubs and trees, purples and reds in profusion. It was a fairly large white building with wide verandahs on three sides. At one end were steps leading to a minaret upon which was a dome, and this was surmounted by the familiar Star and Crescent. It was a Mosque for the Indian troops, who once lived in this area and whose accommodation we are now using. The white-washed interior of the mosque was most attractive, a large central 'nave' revealing the typical Moorish style of architecture in the curiously shaped arches supporting the roof. Between the arches of the nave there was a low wall topped with red tiles and at intervals set into the sides of these walls were some moulded glazed tiles, turquoise in colour, they were pierced to admit a pattern of light. Beyond the low walls were the verandahs roofed with "atap"*. Two gates on wrought-iron hinges gave entry into the building. Beyond the nave was a smaller 'chancel', and the sun was streaming through a vertical line of those turquoise tiles which were set into both sides of this chancel.

When first I entered the Mosque it was bare of furniture except that in the chancel stood what is, I believe, called Allah's Chair, and a cupboard filled with Muslim books. It was obvious immediately that this little Mosque was admirably suitable for a Church. Subsequently as our various ideas and plans have been fulfilled, I am convinced that in this tropical climate, it is a most suitable and sound, as well as aesthetic design for a Christian place of worship, it is both light and pleasantly cool, being open on three sides.

* Atap refers to leaves from a palm tree

Pen and ink drawing by POW Payne of the dome on top of the converted mosque.
Payne wrote: "A spire perhaps would have seemed queerly out of place among the coconuts"

It was not difficult to get permission to use the building, once having this I soon had volunteers, both officers and men, who spent their first Saturday in captivity in making a Church. The results were almost miraculous. In one day, we had made a Church. First the religious books were safely stored away, and the ceremonial chair adapted for temporary use as a pulpit. Next a sideboard from a billet nearby was converted into an Altar raised in two steps. A blue carpet, once part of a marquee, was fixed in the sanctuary, altar rails were roughly built and put into position. Seating was brought from the open-air cinema in the village of Changi. The Altar was furnished with a blue frontal and dorsal curtain, these were made from a piece of an Indian tent, and the colour was excellent.

As you peruse these notes you will read of the improvements and additions which are constantly being made. But even on that first Sunday in Captivity the Church was beautiful and dignified in its simplicity, it amazed us all.

But there are one or two more things that go to produce that picture. We were given two silver candlesticks by a Sergeant-Major who 'found' them during the battle, and for the first few weeks we had a limed oak cross on the Altar. Above the Altar against the white wall is fastened an eight foot Cross, effective in its simplicity. An enormous pitcher stands at the foot of the Chancel, and this is kept full of magnificent purple flowers. A Credence table and a prayer desk were made within a few days. A Muslim book rest and vases of flowers on the Altar complete the picture of the Church.

There is much to be said about the spiritual side of our life here, but first something about some practical needs in the Church, and how we met them.

Eric's pencilled design for metal candlesticks for St George's. On it he writes: "the cup is filled with oil and the flame from the wick is exactly similar to a candle flame."

At first the odd inch of candle which we had retained was fastened in a paper stock and this produced a dignified candle ten inches long, but this was a temporary makeshift. The Ordnance Corps have made two candles to our own "patented" design. Two tubes of tin painted white and properly soldered of the correct length and width have been made from old biscuit tins. These tubes have fitted in the top a little tin cup, just wide enough to fit easily into the tube, the depth of the cup is about one inch. Across the top is a disc of tin with a tiny tube and wick. Into this cup is placed a mixture of old engine oil and paraffin which have been "acquired". They are a tremendous success and even close up are indistinguishable from the real thing.

Pen and ink drawing of St George's Mark 1, the converted mosque in India Lines (previously Indian barracks area), Changi POW Camp. *By POW Stacy 1943*

My main supply of Altar Wine had to be left with our abandoned kit, I had only a small quantity in my field communion set, so for the first Sunday at crowded services I told those present I should use the ancient custom (as I believe it is) of intinction. I consecrated a tiny quantity in the Chalice and then dipped the half wafer into the Chalice and administered direct into the mouth, I did this for two Sundays and had no grouses! As we are ambitious here, we are now making our own wine. We have collected several pounds of raisins. I have not questioned the source of the supply, it is unwise to ask too much about anything which is acquired unusually. But with the help of my Sacristan (incidentally the Supply Officer and an important person), and our Mess Cook (a Server, too), we have produced wine from raisins, which after all is wine from grapes. The recipe is as follows: a mug full of raisins and a pint of water and two large tablespoonsful of our precious sugar. This mixture cooked and strained and left to ferment produces a deep amber wine full of flavour. I have made many bottles of this, and it is excellent and perfectly suitable, we should now be able to last for a long time.

We have our officials, first there are the two Wardens, the Padre's Warden who helped me so much with the Church in its beginnings and a Corporal is People's Warden. One of his jobs is to superintend the carrying of large numbers of forms into Church for Evensong, he has a band of keen 'sidesmen'. Then there is the Sacristan (who hopes to take Orders when we return), and he has trained and is still training a body of Servers who assist at the Altar in the daily Celebration, There is also the Choirmaster (for some months our worthy and first rate Quarter Master) who is an expert at harmony and voice production, and he has a well trained choir of twenty to thirty who practice regularly. The last but very important is the Verger[*], who is my batman, who, besides being a really wonderful batman and excellent fellow, keeps the Church spotless, and is an artist at flowers, and so keeps the sanctuary looking beautiful.

[*] Frederick Stanbury, whose death on the Burma Railway is recorded in the next chapter

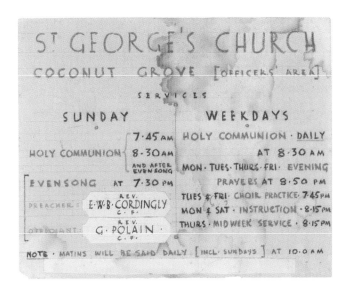

Crayoned notice of the church services taking place at St George's Church,
Coconut Grove in Changi POW Camp.

As I have mentioned each day there is a Celebration of Holy Communion at 8.30 a.m. This late hour is necessary as we are working to Jap time which is an hour and a half later than Malay time. During our first month here we have had between eight and twelve each day and nearly two hundred on Sundays. Then each night we meet in Church at 7.30 p.m. when I give a short talk followed by general discussion and then Compline. The numbers and enthusiasm here is terrific. I have planned a syllabus lasting many months. We are tackling fundamentals, just simple teaching based on the Catechism, and in the absence of any books to assist, I am tackling things in the same way that I did in England in teaching in my own Church School. All sorts of Officers and men attend, and "other denominations" of all brands. We hope for many Confirmation candidates. In addition to these activities several officers and men meet in my tiny room (which in the "piping times" housed the Indian shoemaker). Those who meet in here are men who want to take Orders and together we puzzle out the big things in our faith. The G.O.C.[†] in visiting us at our Service last Sunday 'chipped' me about the "embryo" theological college he had heard was in being, and suggested it should be affiliated to the Divisional University which is the title of the advanced vocational training begun in the Division.

* Compline is the final church service of the day
✝ General Officer Commanding

It is a source of amazement to me and gratitude that up to the present we are permitted to have our large Sunday services, two Celebrations, two parade services of eight hundred each. At the Parade services which are simple but I think inspiring, we finish with the National Anthem. Sung Evensong completes the day, and brings thoughts of home to each one of us. At the beginning we sang our hymns from large sheets of black-out paper fastened up in Church, each of the ten sheets have the hymns chalked on it. But later we had produced several typed sheets of hymns and psalms, these have been duplicated for us.

During the past few days the Senior Chaplain, at the request of the G.O.C. has asked me to be responsible for what is termed the Theological Faculty of our University. I have agreed to do this, but expressed my great limitations, not being a scholar, and having no books. Pressure has been brought to bear from all directions so I have agreed to do my best. I do feel very strongly about the whole matter of men for Ordination, and I have been in touch with the other chaplains and obtained their agreement on our procedure. I am sure that much more is wanted than that a man should be pious and devotional, he must have personality and strength of character and a sound simple faith, and lots of "guts", he should, too, be educated in the widest sense of the term. I have issued a short statement and had it circulated throughout the whole camp giving an outline of our plans. Any man who wishes to test his vocation, and is keen about Orders will be carefully "vetted" by his own padre, and then sent on to me, I feel this responsibility very much. I have compiled a syllabus and a list of lectures. Included in our simple course will be N.T. Greek and Latin under an Officer who recently got a first at Cambridge. We are also tackling New and Old Testament Theology and Dogmatics and Church History under two padres who got good degrees at the University, I follow in the rear with some talks on Prayer Book and Worship.

We hope for really great things from this little theological college. I am giving it my fullest attention, and intend that the atmosphere and devotional side as well as the lectures shall be the finest we can have, perhaps humbly modelling ourselves on "B.K." of Westcott House[*]. When we return to England it is my hope that a dozen to twenty men will be led a little way along the road to Ordination, and we shall certainly be in a position to offer to the competent authority men who have tried their vocation in circumstances of real testing.

* * * *

[*] Rev B.K. Cunningham, Principal of Westcott House, Cambridge, 1919 - 43

I shall hope to be able to convince the reader of what is at present felt by us all, namely a growing religious life centred round our Church of St. George.* No priest could wish for a happier "parish" or sphere of work. Work unfettered by what are sometimes tiresome parish organisations. We seem somehow to have got back to fundamentals and simple wholesome worship, and we all feel the need for a real religion – and all this in spite of the unpleasantness of Captivity, lack of nourishing food, and the tropical heat.

My own life personally is richer by these experiences, and whatever happens to our diet, which is often pretty grim, and however irksome may become our rules and regulations as prisoners, I am sure this experience is something I shall value for ever.

---

* The badge of the Royal Northumberland Fusiliers depicted St George killing the dragon. This may have given Eric the inspiration for his church's name. It was a name to which he remained faithful. In 1960, when he was Rector of a group ministry in Stevenage he oversaw the construction of the largest parish church in England built since the war and he called it St George's.

THE WEATHER

A tropical rainstorm has to be seen to be believed. The rain has been falling down in a sort of superior English cloud burst and has lasted for more than an hour. This has been accompanied by a heavy barrage of thunder and lightning. It is easy to understand how Singapore has ninety inches of rain in a year or seven or eight inches a month. We have had many of these storms during the past weeks. We find them useful as they provide an excellent means of bathing. As soon as the rain falls people come tumbling out of everywhere stripped and begin their strenuous ablutions.

Soon after the rain, the sun will return all its tropical intensity, and we shall "steam", and feel as energetic as patients in a Turkish bath. Strenuous exercise or even walking any distance is a real effort. But for all this the early mornings and late evenings are fairly cool, and even sleeping is reasonably pleasant if no blanket is used and you possess a mosquito net.

A FEAST

It had been a day of much rain, and of depressingly uninteresting diet, just rice with a faint smattering of bits of carrot, I believe one small tin of carrots mixed with four gallons of rice; the other meals were equally dismal, but later four of us were summoned to Sandy's room, for it was his birthday, and here a regal party was held. Wilky, the Doc, Richard, Sandy and myself feasted on a special birthday cake made by the mess staff "under the hat". It was a pastry affair with a sort of chocolate sauce spread on it. This was followed by the sharing of a tin of herrings and a small tin of tongue. Sandy had carried these with him from England for a rainy day, and this had arrived. This really terrific meal, if eaten in rather a primitive fashion, was in the nature of a feast, especially as it was topped with a small swig of rum from the pocket flask of one of the guests. How easily one can feel like a school-boy again, but the party was a great success.

MARCH 1942

The Church was packed for Evensong last night, and half an hour before the service it was impossible to get a seat. For many minutes before the service there is much carrying of forms and seats. All the officers who come bring their own chairs with them. It is an amusing sight to watch men approaching from all directions carrying chairs of all sorts and descriptions, camp chairs, wicker chairs, easy chairs, home-made chairs.

To hear the hymns and psalms and canticles sung by several hundred men and led by a finely trained choir is most inspiring. The choir is really magnificent, and of course, sing unaccompanied, but with simple and rich harmonies. They thrilled us last night with an anthem "Comrades". I am wondering whether to abandon a vague idea I have of attempting to build a small pipe organ. There seems no limit to the ingenuity and "Swiss Family Robinson" activity. There has been installed a pulpit light made from the dashboard light and battery of a broken down car.

Pencil drawing by POW Mike Hardy on which he has written " Padre Cordingly accompanied
by Padre Davidson entering St George's for Evensong, Changi 30.6.42

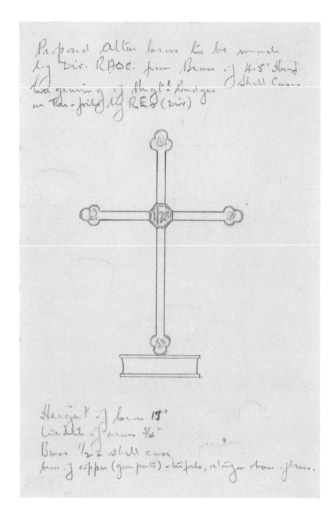

Eric's pencilled design for the new altar cross "to be made by Div. RAOC from brass of 4.5. Howitzer shell case". The cross was made by Sgt Harry Stogden. Eric took it up-country with him to Thailand the following year and brought it back to Changi Prison for his final year as a POW. The cross is now in the Changi Museum Chapel, Singapore.

In order to replace our rather crude and hastily made Altar Cross, we have designed a Cross which has now been made from the brass of a 4.5 Howitzer shell case, and some bits of brass from an ordnance gun shop. The R.A.O.C. have mounted the cross on a half shell case, and there are four trefoils one at the end of each arm, and a craftsman from the Sappers has engraved on the trefoils the badges of the four Regiments in this "parish". The Cross is finished and its workmanship is first rate. Our Altar is now most dignified.

Eric in white (tropical) cassock standing in St George's Mark 1 with the new brass cross on the altar. This photograph was taken by Sergeant Harry Stogden RAOC, the prisoner who had made the cross. Harry Stogden from Pontypridd died, aged 38, from Beri-beri on board the USS Haven on his way home and was buried at sea. The negatives from his camera film survived and this photograph was discovered by his son Bernard in 2007.

It is a bit grim feeling hungry, the rice which, as I have said, forms practically the whole of our diet is satisfying for about an hour after each meal, and after that a certain amount of hunger sets in, it varies, and sometimes one feels almost desperate, and if a chunk of cocoanut can be "scrounged" it is eagerly eaten. I suppose there is not the same nourishment in our present diet, though if we can keep fit, it will not do us a great deal of harm. The "lean and hungry" look is something we must get used to. There are many hundreds of men down with various forms of dysentery, and "tummy " troubles, due, I suppose to the diet and flies.

Yesterday I visited the Hospital which is in the camp area, and occupies a good number of large and damaged blocks. There are well over a thousand of our wounded here and about the same number of sick and dysentery cases. A visit to the wards is rather pitiful and one realises that the aftermath of war is grim. It is hard to imagine the difficulties under which the medical services are staggering. All water has to be carried, no lights are installed. There is a great shortage of medical and surgical kit as well as drugs and medicines.

I spent over two hours visiting the men of my Regiment, and again flies and the diet of rice haunted me. Neither of these things encourages the mending of wounds, and this in addition to the heat and inadequate bedding and ordinary fittings which make a hospital in England seem so clean and fresh and efficient. The staff which is first rate is battling with terrific odds.

It has been necessary to plan an Imperial War Graves' Cemetery. And during the first month over thirty graves were filled, and since then there have often been 2 or 3 funerals a day.

* * * *

The Allied prisoners wired themselves in and organised their own routine and rules. But they were told that anyone seen outside the wire would be shot.

The Japs have decided that we must be "wired in", so it has been done by our own soldiers in our own way and in our own time under our own supervision. During this whole task which has taken about a week, there have been no Japs on the prowl. Personally I have not seen one for several weeks now. We are not getting any special consideration from our captors, and the answer to our urgent request that the men might write home has been met with the reply that the Nippon Army has been on this campaign for several months, they have neither written nor received letters, so why should we be worried and impatient. The oriental mind is very different from our own.

* * * *

After just one month here our "parish" seems consolidated, and now is growing on firm foundations. I really can't express or convey in writing the wonder of the day from a padre's standpoint. The first Celebration was as usual at 8.30 a.m. and our communicants numbered seventy, and these numbers have been increasing steadily each week. This is the more remarkable as a third of the troops have been marched off to Singapore by the Japs to tidy up the town. Then there followed two parade Services, these were parades and not voluntary, but in spite of this there was no fidgeting, and the services went well. Fifty men stayed behind for the second Celebration. Figures are dull, and Christianity isn't a business of counting heads, but let me just add a few more statistics for what they are worth. The average number at the daily Celebrations has been about a dozen, and this number is increasing. Our numbers at Evensong have gone well above the three hundred mark.

Evensong completes the day, except for an officers' discussion group which meets in my room later in the evening. I don't know why Evensong seems so impressive, each week it seems more beautiful, and I know this is the impression we all feel. Perhaps it is the simplicity of it coupled with the thoughts that at home this same service, chants, hymns are being sung. I am sure that the use of an organ at our service would be almost sacrilegious. There is no bawling, and it must have rivalled the efforts of a community like Kelham or the Cowley Fathers[*].

After the Service more men came forward for Confirmation, and our preparation class is now over three dozen. Since we have no Bishop available, I am taking the rubric at the end of the Confirmation Service literally; that none shall be admitted to Holy Communion unless he be confirmed or "ready and desirous of being confirmed".

These men want to be confirmed, and seem very disappointed when one explains how impossible it is at present. I am preparing them for their first Communion on Easter Day, which is three weeks ahead, but in our life much can be done in that time.

The daily evening talks, followed by discussion and Compline continue with the same enthusiasm, and the Church is invariably filled to capacity. The faces vary a bit, and I often wonder what makes them come; a fortnight of hard work on the Sacraments might at home be thought a bit frightening, but here it hasn't proved to be so.

* * * *

The work of St George's Church is made so much easier by the help given by the officers, both senior and junior, and one feels so very grateful to them.

In the General[+] commanding our Division we have a really fine Christian gentleman. Never have I met a layman who has been so keen on the work of a padre. He supports everything that is done and is often to be seen at the weekday Celebrations. His encouragement and interest helps so tremendously, because one knows his religion is a big essential in his life. Time after time in discussion with him I have felt how really and truly the facts of Christianity are a part of his life. No man can have done more in this part of the camp for the spiritual, mental and physical welfare of those under his command.

---

* Anglican religious orders
+ Maj-General Merton Beckwith-Smith was known affectionately as "Becky." In August 1942 he was sent with other senior officers to Japanese-occupied Taiwan and died there three months later.

After a very disturbed couple of nights I have succumbed to the prevalent "Tummy trouble", a mild sort of dysentery. One feels awfully weak through it, and this is aggravated by a starvation diet of liquids only, no rice is allowed. The "doc" has promised to have me fit in a day or so, and I have insisted on this as Holy Week and Easter are only a few days away. His dope of Bismuth and chloroform or some similar concoction seems to be working wonders. I have been overwhelmed during the day by the kindnesses and practical comradeship of everyone here. First the gift of two packets of cigarettes, a treat and a sacrifice because they are practically non existent. (Cigarettes can occasionally be smuggled into the camp and cost ten dollars for fifty which is about twenty-five shillings). Officers and men have been drifting in and out all day. The various members of the mess staff whom I have known so well for two years, have brought me several mugs of real tea with a really generous dose of tinned milk and sugar in it. How one does appreciate these simple oddments, which are to us almost unheard of luxuries.

* * * *

I am anxious to make Holy Week and Easter a big event for all of us here. We have a great advantage in that we can appeal to the keeping of these days at home, and the link we shall have with those we love. I had thought that those preparing for Confirmation would like to meet for about three afternoons a week. I put this proposition forward at our first instruction and the unanimous cry was for a daily talk. I pleaded that "spiritual indigestion" might be the result, but that excuse was ignored. We meet daily and there is a fine spirit growing up in this group, I hope for big things from these men.

APRIL 1942

Fate and the Japs did their best to spoil our plans for Easter, and a further six hundred men were sent off to Singapore during Holy Week, and with them went quite a number of the Confirmation Candidates, and more than half of the choir. This meant abandoning our efforts for a sung Eucharist on Easter Day, and also modifying our ambitious plans for the festival.

In spite of these things Easter has been an amazing revelation. The Holy Week services of Holy Communion in the morning and Compline and a talk in the evening prepared us for Good Friday. That day began with Mattins and Ante-Communion at 8.30 a.m. and was packed as were all the services during the day. We said the Litany at noon, and a nearby padre conducted a devotional service at 2 o'clock, and we finished with Evensong just before nightfall.

In the best traditions we decorated the Church on the Saturday, and covered the Altar with vases of beautiful white flowers (Frangiapania) like a large white gardenia, and it is the most sweet smelling flower on the island. We had huge pots of other flowers in the chancel.

Easter morning began with Holy Communion just as it was getting light at 8 a.m., and four other Celebrations followed at three-quarter hourly intervals. Those prepared for Confirmation made their Communion corporately during the morning, with nearly five hundred others.

I felt somehow that here in our regular life away from the rush and bustle of the world outside, we had captured the atmosphere of the week. Good Friday and Easter Day stood out so clearly in our life here and the contrast was noticed and felt by us all.

One constantly hears such a remark as – "You know St George's Church means so much to me". It has become the focal point of much of our life here. It is mentioned at Divisional and Area Conferences, it is a landmark, "The new water-point is situated opposite St. George's Church", reads Camp Orders. "No water will be carried during services" quotes another, and so on in a dozen similar ways.

So this little ex-mosque, in a small degree similar to its famous predecessor in Constantinople, St. Sophia, is much more than an attractive building. In such a short space of time it has assumed a tremendous and not exaggerated importance, and has attracted so many people. At any hour of the day there are to be seen thirty or forty men reading and writing or just resting under the roof of this Church, which still has firmly fastened on the top of its dome the familiar Moslem Star and Crescent. A week or so after writing these notes, on a wet afternoon a little bearded Indian arrived on the pillion of a motorcycle. He came straight to me where I was busy giving a talk in Church. He introduced himself as the Moslem priest whose mosque we were now using. He had come for his prayer books, which fortunately I had saved and kept hidden in my cupboard. He was overjoyed to receive them, and in 'pidgin' English we introduced each other as 'padres' of religion. He rather surprised me with his broadminded remark that he was glad that I was using his building, and that it was being used for the worship of God. It appeared that he too had lived in my room, or rather that I was now occupying his room – "The Shoe-maker's Room", so I suppose the little priest combined shoemaking with his religious duties. This was a most pleasing encounter, and reminded me of an equally friendly Moslem priest at the camp in India, who was a tailor and who wanted to make my white cassock as a gift from one "padre-sahib" to another. I remember telling him that I wished my people were as regular and careful over saying their prayers as his were. I think we have quite a bit to learn about our duty to worship. We are inclined to put all our emphasis on Christ's second command and ignore "the first and great commandment".

Sitting in my little room in the sweltering heat of an April afternoon, and looking beyond the Church to the sea a mile away, I wonder as we all do, how long this captivity will last, will it be months or years? How will it all end, and how shall we be released? We get no news of the world and the war, except fantastic rumours, too startling and optimistic even to contemplate. The days pass quickly enough, for most of us have as much work as we can tackle, yet it seems that we have been here a very long time. I suppose this is due to our regular daily routine and the familiarity of our surroundings, and the absence of news of the most important things in our lives – our homes and our families.

The home link is very strong, and reaches its peak, probably in conditions such as ours. Hardly half an hour passes in a day without a visitor knocking on my door wishing to discuss some problem of home and family and faith and works.

In spite of personal loneliness I am convinced that all is well with my home and my wife and two sons. One develops a terrific faith in these things. Like the majority of folk here I have not received a letter from England since we left, the chance of any mail now is remote.

Tempers are short and a sense of humour is a prized possession. There is not a lot of laughter, but conditions are rather against a robust humour, but there is a grand sense of comradeship.

* * * *

Drawing of the Cookhouse by POW Mike Hardy 28.6.42 on which he has written: "From where had come so many things nice, But now, an endless stream of rice." Many new recipes to disguise the rice were attempted by the ingenious cooks including a highly successful rice porridge and 'ersatz' coffee made from roasted rice.

Food is still one of the major considerations each day, and we live from meal to meal. Never has food assumed such vital proportions. Naturally it forms one of the main topics of talk and provides ample scope for grouses and criticism. Many new recipes for the treatment and camouflage of rice are being tried, among them is a highly successful porridge made of ground rice, and also an 'ersatz' coffee made from roasted rice. The latter is quite palatable and not unlike coffee.

Once a month we have bread from our own camp bakery. It is a much looked-forward-to treat, and is made on the sour dough principle. I believe it is the Biblical way of making bread by using some of the previous day's dough, which has fermented, to "leaven the lump" or new dough.

* * * *

As is well known there is no twilight on the Equator. The sun is shining just after eight o'clock in the morning, but it is quite dark half an hour before. In the evening there is a short sunset and darkness follows very quickly, it is dark at half past eight. In consequence our evenings are long and sometimes a little dreary, we have no lamps nor electric light at present, so that reading and cards are impossible after sunset. It is not quite as grim as it might appear as there are several "Heath Robinson" lamps in being, made from cigarette tins with broken bottles as lamp glasses. The fuel has as its basis the almost indispensable old engine oil.

Padre's Room. Eric's room in Changi POW Camp. This room had earlier belonged to the Moslem priest whose mosque was converted into St George's. It was also called the Shoe-Maker's room because the Indian priest had combined shoe-making with his religious duties. *Pencil drawing by POW Mike Hardy 26.6.42*

Among minor unpleasantness are bugs. I don't mean the familiar, or rather, better known, bed bug, this creature is a familiar pest and a real problem, one is continually combating them. My "bete noir" is the cockroach. An evening or so ago my room was stormed by dozens of these brutes, large brown beetle-like creatures, between two and three inches long, covered with excellent armour-plating, capable of astounding bursts of speed, and 'in extremis' able to fly a yard or two. After a battle lasting nearly an hour I had a couple of dozen corpses, but these casualties did not represent the annihilation of their forces as lots fled. Preparing to get to bed I was amazed to find there were several large grasshoppers leaping about and two enormous spiders occupying good positions on the wall. Defeated I retired hastily onto the bed and securely fastened the mosquito netting round the mattress. A cowardly act, perhaps, but I felt quite unable to combat further the "long leggety beasties" with only a slipper and a feeble torch light.

* * * *

THE UNIVERSITY

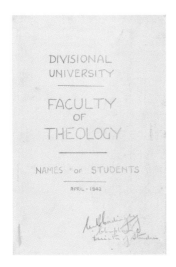

DIVISIONAL
UNIVERSITY

FACULTY
OF
THEOLOGY

NAMES OF STUDENTS

APRIL - 1942

Cover of a book made by Eric
for the Faculty of Theology
of the Camp's new Divisional
University. Nearly 30 students
enrolled for this course.

Fuller mention must be made of the University. After many meetings and much planning, it has now emerged as a properly organised body with its faculties and staffs of lecturers. There are faculties in a variety of subjects, Modern Languages, English Language and Literature, History, Mathematics, Economics, Geography, and the "Queen of the Sciences" Theology. In about a month's time it is hoped to open faculties in Military History, Agriculture and Music. The Heads of various subjects have met several times and time tables and a syllabus in each subject has been prepared. The lecturers are all university men, and they are excused all military duties. Each Faculty has between six and ten lectures a week, and the lectures are held either in our Church of St. George, or in the Officers' Mess. The response from the officers and men in the Division has been excellent, and candidates number from 25 to 150 in each subject. Each student is interviewed by the Head of the Faculty and the membership to the University is limited to those who have attained matriculation standard. Even though at present no text books are available, the standard of the lectures is exceedingly high, and the keenness and enthusiasm is remarkable.

The Theological Faculty for which I am responsible is, naturally, rather smaller than some others but we number nearly thirty students. Of this number there are some who are reading one or more subjects because they are interested in the subject chosen. But as I have mentioned earlier on, within this number there is a smaller group who are reading the whole course with a view to Ordination after the war. The number of "embryo" Ordinands is eighteen and among these there is some excellent material, and I am sure some first-rate future parish priests.

I wonder if there have ever before been prisoners of war who have organised their own University and been able to attend a planned course of lectures such as we are doing. As the students stream from one lecture to another, and one listens to the fragments of conversation, one is reminded again of the typical atmosphere which is a part of the life in our universities at home. I feel that our privilege is unique, and I have so often laboured this point, our whole life in captivity is strange and odd. Perhaps we do not appreciate our freedom of thought and our restricted freedom of movement that is allowed us, or perhaps our captors are too busy elsewhere to bother much with us ?

I feel all this is too good to last, and I dread the time that may come *and did come* (Eric has inserted this in pencil) when we are all split up into labour gangs and sent to various parts. Many parties of men have marched off to Singapore during the past weeks, but I hope that we shall be allowed to continue our full and varied life here.

MAY 1942

Our life of late has been obsessed with a frantic talk about Vitamins. Never had I imagined could those nebulous things have assumed such vast importance. I suppose it all began with an analysis of our rice diet. It appears that rice is nearly all carbo-hydrates, and that by washing it many times to make it less gritty and more palatable this destroys the minute quantity of Vitamin B there should be in unpolished rice. Then there has been a scare of beri-beri, which is, I believe a disease brought about by a diet such as ours, and due to the lack of Vitamin B in the food. Orientals and those who live mainly on rice suffer from beri-beri if they eat polished or finished rice. From Vitamin B the medical people began to work out the Vitamin content in our food, and soon the whole camp was discussing Vitamins as though they were some new delicacy we should seek. Each article of food was the subject of debate, and its value in vitamins was assessed. As we do not get any fresh vegetables, we are short of Vitamin C, and we seem to get practically no supplies of A and D, it has been said that we are living on a diet which it is impossible to live on! Our Doc. has said that this is a vast experiment and most valuable as it will teach the medical profession much about Vitamins, as the whole subject is virtually in its infancy. It may be an interesting experiment, but it is a monotonous one, and one I hope we shall survive. I have just heard that there are 150 cases of beri-beri in the hospital, and that even the Japs are worried, and have sent a quantity of Vitamin B tablets for these patients. They have also intimated that they will really give us four ounces of fresh fruit or vegetables each day. At present the only change in our diet has been the cutting out of our tinned milk, this much prized article did, we understand, provide a few of these needed Vitamins.

Beri-beri is not our only worry, the chief cause for alarm is dysentery, and there are several blocks in the hospital tackling this complaint. Casualties have been heavy, and 26 men were buried in four days, and half the number of fatalities are from dysentery.

At present malaria is not prevalent, there are some men down with it, but I think our precautions are adequate to avoid an epidemic. Men are constantly clearing out the anti-malarial drains and no pools of water are allowed to become breeding places for mosquitoes. We understand that neither dysentery nor malaria existed on this island before the recent battle, owing to the excellent preventative measures that were in existence before our captivity.

* * * *

We have thought for some time that this life here was a little too good to last, and it now appears that there is a determined effort to break up the ordered life of the many thousands in camp here. For some weeks now parties of officers and men have been drafted off and sent to various work on the island. Lately it has seemed that every three or four days demands for more men have come. My "parish" has suffered in consequence, a good many of the units left are at "skeleton" strength, and I am now responsible for the remnant of the five Gunner Regiments. Though this exodus will affect our work here, my parish is still flourishing as it now is responsible for many more units. I have now over eighty men on the register for Confirmation, but many of this number are forced to leave with their course of preparation only partially completed. Every few days a group of men will come into my room to say goodbye, their thanks and gratitude are really touching. The Church, they say, has meant so much to them, it has given them a new vision and ideal. Though for some their contact with our great little centre has been short, I am convinced its effect will live in their lives very much in the future. The numbers at the daily Eucharist have risen to nearly twenty a day, though I must be prepared for a decrease in this number as men are sent off to Singapore.

I hope so much that we are allowed to continue the work and life here, but that will depend on our captors.

Our Church is progressing in its improvements., We have now carpeted the nave with new cocoanut matting, given by a Commanding Officer. The Sappers are busy making some Altar Rails which are simple yet beautiful in design and workmanship, and really worthy of the building.

Whilst some of my Unit were on a working party in Singapore they were able to get sent up here a dilapidated and badly damaged harmonium. It was a wheezy and broken down affair with half its notes out of order and most of its inside loose and worn out. It has now been completely rebuilt and overhauled, so that it works perfectly, but more than that, it is fitted out with a brand new case, and it is a far better and stronger instrument than when new. These efforts are samples of the keenness and devotion which is shown by so many.

Hundreds, but I think it will be thousands of men will have cause to be grateful to St George's, and I am sure will speak with pride of their connection with this little one-time mosque. Its influence is something which has grown not through human efforts, but the work of the Holy Spirit. We seem to live again the simple enthusiasm and vitality of the "Acts". That I feel is the most accurate description of this life, perhaps those at home would not believe this possible, but it must be remembered that we are separated from so much that was artificial in life, and the comparison is a true one.

Last Sunday was a memorable day in that I baptised three men, two officers and a lance corporal. It was an impressive little service, the font was rigged up from an ancient mortar or flour grinder, and placed in the back of the Church. Each Candidate had two sponsors and in the quiet of the morning this solemn sacrament of "Baptism for those of Riper Years" was read from the Prayer Book. It has been my privilege to baptise many men as the weeks pass. Hardly a Sunday passes without a Baptism.

* * * *

Several POWs died each week in the Camp, often from preventable diseases caused by the starvation diet and lack of adequate medicine. *Pencil drawing of a funeral procession by POW Mike Hardy*

One of the saddest and most distressing parts of a padre's life here concerns funerals. Often I have officiated at five and six in a week. It is made more poignant because the deaths nowadays are mainly from dysentery, a preventable and quite unnecessary disease. The funerals are always well carried out and are military in character. A hundred or so men will be on parade, wreaths will have been made, a bugler is there. Standing at the entrance of the newly constructed military cemetery, just outside our wired-in camp, it is an impressive sight to see this column of men slow marching behind the wheeled stretcher on which rests the body wrapped in a blanket and draped in a Union Jack. Six graves are always ready for use, and a funeral takes place the same day as the death. It sometimes happens that a person you have spoken to is buried by you a day or so later. There is real meaning in those words from the Burial Service "in the midst of life we are in death".

The Cemetery is carefully planned and in its simple dignity looks quite beautiful, set out with the grassed banks, flower beds, hedges and shrubs and gravelled paths. A few weeks ago this same area had been a rough jungle undergrowth. In straight lines there are standing 400 (*150 has been crossed out and 400 inserted in pencil*) wooden crosses, as these increase week by week the grim thought comes into one's mind that many of these crosses cover the mortal remains of men reported safe after battle. Men who need not have died but for the facts and conditions of our captivity.

* * * *

Funeral Procession. Eric officiated at many funerals and wrote: "It is an impressive
sight to see this column of men slow marching behind the wheeled stretcher on
which rests the body wrapped in a blanket and draped in a Union Jack."
Pen and ink drawing of a funeral procession by POW Payne

Even those folk who have never lived in the tropics are familiar with the typical landscape of the East. The films and photographs have given glamour to the scene of palm trees and exotic plants and the brilliant colours of the flowering trees. Bright sunshine, sudden rainstorms, gigantic butterflies, and then the breathless nights with the continuous buzzing of insects, and the moon clear and bright casting long shadows over this scene; such is often the romantic setting of film and novel, and such is the setting of our prison life. It will be understood when I say that the glamour and romance has ceased to appeal to us tremendously, for most, rain in a mean back street in Manchester would have at the moment a far greater appeal.

A prisoner's life in a hot climate has perhaps one advantage in the matter of clothes. Officers and men arrived in this camp in their shorts and shirts of battle, some possessed a few extras stuffed into packs and haversacks. The majority have continued to wear this "two-piece" outfit, though a few have succeeded in acquiring a spare set. Laundering presents no real problems as the sun dries the cloth in an hour or two. The men are forbidden to wear shirts during the day, and their tanned bodies would be the envy of many modern sun bathers. Shorts and shirts have though a distinct disadvantage in the long evenings as more flesh is exposed to the bites of ants and mosquitoes.

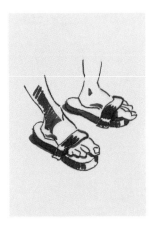

When their shoes wore out
the prisoners made clogs
with canvas straps and
wooden soles.

The clatter of home-made wooden clogs is now a familiar noise in and around the buildings in camp. These buildings, which house so many of us are two storey modern concrete erections, and in our area used to be the barracks of the Indian garrison on the island. Solid and well constructed are these buildings, and the Officers' Mess which is next to the Church sleeps seventy Officers on the first floor and twenty-five downstairs. This ground floor is divided into two sections with a canvas screen, and on the one side we all feed together. It is rather like a typical barrack room with a dozen trestle tables and forms. There is not much comfort, but it is adequate and suitable. The cutlery and china is mixed, and consists of the remnants of the various messes, though much of the stuff had been brought up here from houses in Singapore that had served as headquarters for the various battalions during the battle. Tea is served from silver teapots and from enamel jugs into Royal Worcester cups and pewter tankards and enamel and tin mugs. Our own waiters serve at meal times, and an odd table here and there is furnished with a linen or lace cloth or table mats, whilst others are made colourful with pots of flowers.

For several weeks it has been usual for groups of men to get together during the evening for an alfresco meal. Perhaps a dish of rice had been put aside or a slice of our too rare bread, or a rice biscuit saved. These oddments of food garnished with some tinned pilchards or pine apple or a little jam and washed down with some brewed tea made from water begged from the cookhouse, has brightened our evenings and added to our slender diet. We have been very fortunate in receiving small parcels of tinned food from the working parties in Singapore. Herrings, cheese, jam, "bully" beef, sardines, these tins have done much to make up for a lack of nourishing foods in our rations.

JUNE 1942

Whitsunday has passed, it was another milestone in our life here, and we shall remember it. After a lot of practice we sang the Eucharist, Merbecke's* traditional setting of the Prayer Book Service had been remembered by various people and put onto manuscript. The Service was packed, and the communicants at this and the other Celebrations amounted to nearly three hundred.

Up to late on the evening before, the Sappers had worked to finish a magnificent set of Altar Rails. Simple but finely and solidly proportioned one would scarcely believe that it was possible to produce such workmanship in a prison camp. Tools are scarce, wood hard to come by, and no proper workshop, and the hundred and one fittings that make up the ordinary carpenter's shop.

The Church is now electrically lit for Evensong by the installation of several cunningly concealed car headlamps, each throwing a soft reflected light from the white ceiling of the building. Two more hidden lamps floodlight the Altar. The power for our lighting comes from two car batteries, which are kept charged for us, in the recently erected power house in the camp.

The Church was again filled to capacity for an early Sung Eucharist on the festival of Corpus Christi. The Service began as the sun was rising above the clumps of cocoanut trees, and finished in time for the daily queuing up by the men for their breakfast boiled rice. The few persons ignorant of our 'goings-on' made frantic enquiries about the singing coming from the Church at such an early hour, they were easily answered.

* John Merbecke c.1510–1585

Perhaps one of my biggest thrills is to record the hundredth candidate to be prepared for Confirmation. In the four months of our captivity, I have run continuously courses for Confirmation. As soon as one preparation has finished we embark immediately on another, and there has been no shortage of persons. I have invited others to come as well and these "refresher" courses prove most popular. Reviewing these classes, two things stand out. First the eagerness, the intense keenness of men to learn the facts of the faith, and secondly the appalling ignorance of the simplest things of Christianity. Nothing can be taken for granted, this is literally true. I often wonder if we padres do any real teaching. I am sure that the clergy have failed in their first duty of teaching. The substance of so much of our public utterances has been the giving of encouraging talks, just "pi-jaws"[*] and platitudes, instead of the rocks which make the firm and rugged foundation of Christianity.

* * * *

As the end of the first University term approaches I marvel to think what has been accomplished. Lectures have continued throughout the afternoons of the weeks that have passed. In my own Faculty the seven subjects have made real progress, the lecturers have reached a really high standard in their subjects. The whole conception of the University as a whole, and the Faculty of Theology in particular has been so well worth while. I wish I could convey the keenness and enthusiasm there is among the students. As I write these words the students are streaming from the Church having just finished a lecture on the History of English Literature. The Theological students, standing under the verandah of the Church are awaiting the lecturer on New Testament Theology. Here in this equatorial island in the midst of the biggest war the world has known, these soldiers, deprived of their first task of defending their homes and the empire, are turning to things of peace. The pen has replaced the sword, though the time may yet come when that sword will be in their hands again.

* moralising talk

St George's became a centre for social activity, not just for religious services and it hosted a number of Careers Talks in a series "How and Where will you Educate your Son?"

So the weeks pass, and Sunday comes round very quickly, it is the welcome break in the routine of the week. On a special Sunday in June, the day when 28 Nations in the world were united in prayer, we too packed tightly in our hundreds in our little Church, to share with Christians everywhere in worship and prayer. We all felt the significance of this solemn service, and I am sure that each person present in his own way made a real and humble contribution to that day. Our prayers could bridge the ten thousand miles which separates us from those at home, of such I think were our thoughts.

The first page of Eric's handwritten sermon entitled Prayers for POWs, which he preached in Changi on Trinity XX 18.10.42

SERMON: PRAYERS FOR P.O.Ws

Changi – Parade Trinity XX 18/10/42

In a few hours time the Churches in our land will begin to fill with people. Perhaps your picture is of a Church sandwiched between rows of houses – perhaps close to factories or near to shop windows – perhaps it is one that stands so close to the fields, its tower or spire overshadowing the cluster of cottages that make up your village.

In our ancient Cathedrals with organ and choir and in the little wood and tin-roofed Mission Halls with harmonium and worn seating – people in the land we love will be arriving for the Early Service – for Holy Communion – so that they may say their prayers for us and those like us.

Chiefest among those going to Church today will be those nearest and dearest to us whose whole thought will be for you – each one of you. To some small circle of folk at home you mean so much – just everything.

Never in the history of wars has a day been put aside specially for those who are captives. Our King has ordered this day for the nation's prayers to Almighty God for prisoners of war and those from whom they are separated.

They will shortly join with our fellow countrymen in prayer for us. Unknown to them we are able, thank God, to begin this day which for them is still night, in offering our prayers for them.

You do say your prayers don't you – you don't believe that prayers are just fanciful – look round you. There's a lot that you or I or those far cleverer than us can't explain about God and His plans – but don't fuss for miracles and wonder working – look at yourself.

It is almost a year since we sailed from England and yet we are fed and clothed – Red Cross food is worth thanking God for. If we were spirited home this instant – we could only look back on these past months and to God say thank you.

Except for the few who are solid bone from the neck upwards I am convinced that in honest and sobre thought – you are worth more to your fellows and to God in character and experience than that same khaki clad figure that staggered up the gangway last October. But I am wandering – in a moment I want you to say some prayers with me for those at home.

Together today then a great force of prayer will be turned to God – let us see to it that the quality of that prayer is right – not a cringing "it's not fair" sort of attitude – not a selfish plea of pity – but simply a <u>brave trust in a God who is Good</u>.

Prayers are not … to a cruel and angry God – God loathes this useless sacrifice and suffering – all He longs for is that His people should come down on His side – should range themselves alongside Him – help Him to overcome the foulness of war.

Remember the stark beastliness of war is more personal than the wiliness of Nazis and Fascists and war-mongering of men – the hard part – the shattering part for God is that great drag on the wheel which is applied by Christians in their callous little selfishnesses – their inability to serve God. Their open support for the forces of evil which are doing their damnedest to wreck God's cause for a decent world of peace and brotherhood.

Praying to God with your tongue in your cheek – and plodding through a day lived niggardly, selfishly, egotistically isn't aiding God's cause – it is simply heaving a heavy spanner in the works. Saying prayers and living certain kinds of life must fit together – the one without the other is absurd, useless.

We can do so much here – and <u>are we</u>? Or is it the heaving of a spanner – look at that spanner – perhaps it has <u>your name on it</u>.

* * * *

There have been two recent innovations in our Church life here; the first was a small retreat or quiet morning which was arranged for the Ordinands. We spent the morning in Church in prayer and meditation on one of the Ember Days before Trinity. We followed the usual order, we began with Mattins and then there were three addresses with periods of quiet between, and we finished with the Litany. This was the strangest retreat I have yet conducted, because all round us the ordinary routine of life was going on. The washing of clothes, the grinding of rice, the repairing of cookhouses, we could see and hear it all. I was fearful of getting any atmosphere, but oddly enough these familiar noises did not disturb us at all.

The other fact which is so fine was a request from the men for a service of prayer before lights-out each evening. The day has usually finished with Compline said after the daily talks and discussions, but this request was rather different. In the huts and tents and odd billets occupied by the men, there is little privacy or suitable environment for private prayers.

Each evening then at nine o'clock the Church is dimly lit with the Altar candles, and a small flood light on the Altar Cross, and the Church is packed with dim crouching or kneeling forms. It is not a service, I simply announce the special intention we have kept during the day and observed at the Eucharist, and then we say our own prayers, and are occupied with our own thoughts for ten minutes. After these few minutes I say several prayers summing up our thoughts, and give the Blessing, and slip quietly out of the building,

It is rather wonderful, nothing is planned nor spectacular, merely the very real need of the men fulfilled in an atmosphere of quietness which is what they had lacked and desired.

* * * *

The predictions of the pessimists have remained unrealised, and more, they have been confounded. These odd folk who exist, but do not flourish in a prison camp, assured us that conditions would deteriorate as the weeks passed. We are in our eighteenth week and life has improved immensely. The camp is now equipped by our own Sappers with running water, and this means showers and plenty of washing water, a boon in this climate. Recently canteen supplies were sent up and distributed to those who still possessed money. This has meant that the weekly issue of nine or ten cigarettes may occasionally be supplemented by the purchase of Chinese and native cigarettes. A powerful and rather fearsome weed, but a real solace to the heavy smoker. The biggest and latest thrill is the money which we have received from the Japanese Government. We are paid at the daily rate of 25 cents for officers, 15 cents for the N.C.O.s and 10 cents for other ranks, which at the old rate of exchange amounted to sevenpence, fourpence and threepence respectively, though the purchasing value of the Straits dollar has shrunk considerably since the capitulation.

In a few days we are to be issued with a postcard, on which we may write a few simple phrases, this will be the first personal effort to send news to those at home.*

Life is very good, and our position could be so very much worse, we have cause for very real gratitude.

---

* His wife, Mary, received a card on which Eric had written five words, "*Read Second Epistle of John v 12*" : Having many things to write unto you, I would not write with paper and ink : but I trust to come unto you, and speak face to face, that our joy may be full."

"The usual full church for the Padre's Evening Discussions".
Pencil drawing by POW Mike Hardy 3 June 42

After many, many weeks here the daily evening discussions still thrill me, they too have formed such an important contribution to our Church life. On a Friday evening after supper the Church will be filled with men for our weekly "question time". On previous week-days the talk and discussion has followed a prearranged programme ranging from talks on Holy Communion to the Christian attitude to various social problems. Friday is the day for "loose ends" and odd questions.

Having seated myself in the chancel, the questions follow in rapid succession. "Why are the two Lord's Prayers different in Evensong, and why is one shorter than the other?" The next question is probably too big to answer on the spot, "What is the difference between the beliefs of the various Churches?" That question is then split into its obvious parts and dealt with on subsequent evenings. Then there follows a medley of "old favourites", "What does IHS stand for?" Why should we eat fish on Fridays? Are Sunday and the Sabbath the same? What is a mitre? What is the difference between Rector and Vicar, Curate and Dean?" and so on. Then there are sure to be some "hardy annuals", "What is the difference between 'High' and 'Low'"?

This question is a favourite, and comes up under various colours most weeks. The question is usually coupled with a graphic description of some extra "high" or violently "low" practice the questioner has witnessed at home or on his travels. At first the most common questions concerned God and the war, suffering and free-will, but I think at last such thoughts as one is able to give are having the desired effect. It is during these questionings, and even more so in the personal talks with the rather shy after the meeting, or in my room, that one feels so deeply the searching after knowledge, and only too often the abysmal ignorance that exists in what are, to instructed Church people, simple matters of faith and order. The discussion is put aside after three-quarters of an hour, and together we say a simple form of Compline.

That completes what has been one of the daily experiences of camp life, the numbers and faces vary, but the interest and keenness is constant. The majority of those present are, or rather were, not regular churchgoers, and the questions are varied and outspoken. The atmosphere is good and there is no bickering. Men are anxious to get answers to their questions, and keen to give their comments in the general discussion. It is often a real tonic, and not without its humorous side. The men are quite outspoken in their criticism of organised religion, but they are not destructive, they have ideas. It is humbling to realise one's personal limitations. Never again shall I assume that everybody knows what Whitsunday stands for, or the meaning of the phrases from the Creed "He descended into hell".

It is not difficult to preach to the packed congregations Sunday by Sunday, because one has always to answer the intensely practical questions that crop up daily in living in such close contact with men. Such thoughts as – "Can one be a Christian and not go to Church? How can one make sure prayers are real" are among one's thoughts for sermons.

Then any person who for a moment imagines that the Prayer Book Services of Mattins and Evensong are outworn and need modernising and popularising, is, I am sure, quite mistaken. Time and again one hears how much these ordered services do really satisfy that instinct we each have for public worship. Many Nonconformists have said that they have learnt to love the simple plan of the Daily Offices. The Magnificat and Nunc Dimittis are loved, as is the whole service. Obviously chants and all music should be "singable" by the congregation, and all tunes must be set low enough for the range of the ordinary male voice. Everything that goes to make up the service should be planned to satisfy that instinct for worship, and so arranged that each man feels he can join fully in the worship, and that the hymns, prayers and sermon are allied to his living of the days from Monday to Saturday.

A day in this life behind the wire begins as the sun rises above and pierces the dense palm grove to the East of the Church. It is a rush of gold and crimson out of the east. This sudden glare of sunshine strikes through the open door of my room, and no other Reveille is needed. A wash and a shave while the morning is still cool is refreshing, and within a few minutes clad in white cassock I cross the twenty odd yards to Church for the daily Celebration. A server will have already collected from my cupboard those things necessary for the service.

As halfpast eight approaches the Church becomes dotted with those who have come to share in the worship. Life in camp is hardly astir, it is only just daylight. As the little ex-mosque fills one is conscious of the many sorts that make up the morning congregation. A soldier here and there wearing only a ragged pair of shorts, and at his side a mess tin, he will have to hurry out at nine o'clock to join the queue for breakfast. Present too are several officers, and quite often a senior officer, perhaps our own General.

The Server, either officer or other rank, will have prepared the Altar, and lit the little oil lamp candles and so the Service begins. Each man with his own thoughts and prayers, but all remembering the special thought or intention for the day.

After the Celebration and during the half-hour which precedes our breakfast, it is enjoyable to sit in the quiet of this open-sided building and read Mattins. The only noise apart from the birds comes from the stropping of razors and from the more enthusiastic singing over their morning shower. Breakfast of rice porridge and boiled rice and gravy follow, and by ten o'clock both officers and men are off to their various jobs of the day. It must be remembered that our watches are set to Tokio time which is one and a half hours ahead of the local Malay time, so the ten o'clock finish of breakfast is really only half-past eight.

I usually walk round my "parish" for an hour; more often than not work is proceeding in one of the sheds on some object or improvement for the Church. Back to my room where I am kept fully busy preparing addresses and the hundred and one jobs that need preparation and organising. During these two hours one can be certain of half a dozen visitors. Queries and questions, points in Confirmation instruction that need clearing up. The clatter of persons making for the mess room remind one that lunch is ready, and so a similar meal to breakfast is consumed, a pot of jam or some sauce has helped to flavour the food. A discussion of rumours and a native cigarette or cigar rounds off lunch. Large quantities of milkless unsweetened tea, cold or cool make a very refreshing drink, and after one has got used to it, is quite pleasant.

Afternoons are spent in university lectures, interviews, hospital visits, and only too often funerals. It is intensely hot in the sun, but in spite of our lack of topees, wandering through the camp does not result in sunstroke. No longer do we have to rely on rain for bathing, and at six o'clock I make for the showers, and so we assemble again for supper at half-past six. Strenuous efforts will have been made to make the meal attractive, and whenever the rations have permitted those efforts have been successful. A pastry made of rice flour, and perhaps a "cream doughnut" cunningly produced with only rice and oil and sugar and margarine.

Immediately after supper I cross the flagged path to the Church which is filled for the evening discussion or Confirmation instruction. This is one of the high spots of the day, and I really enjoy the discussions of matters of faith and works. We smoke our "farthing" native cigars, and the three-quarters of an hour soon slips away. I have described rather more fully the sort of thing that happens before we kneel to say Compline. The Church empties and off the men go to roll-call. The next half an hour passes pleasantly discussing some point with the odd one or two. Within ten minutes or so it is quite dark, and as nine o'clock is sounded on the camp bell, we cross to the Church again for prayers. I have written of this earlier, the Church is dimly lit with a small flood light onto the Altar, and for ten minutes we are silent in our own private devotions, then final simple prayers on the thought with which we began the day, perhaps for those fighting on our behalf, for the sick and wounded, and then the Blessing.

Then unless there is a sermon or talk to be finished, and unfortunately this only too often occurs, the lighted mess will be the scene of a delightfully scrappy meal. You will remember the oddments that go to make this meal one that is so appreciated. Discussion or reading fills in the hour before lights-out, and so back to my room, where so often I seem to have to destroy the 'beasts of the night', such loathsome crawling and jumping and flying insects, though in a few minutes I feel safe behind the screening of a mosquito net. So ends a day that is I suppose typical, though each one is so varied and so full that its description would be far beyond my limited powers. Perhaps the reader will understand that for many of us, and certainly a padre, the life is not dull nor boring, the days and weeks have passed so quickly. It has not been irksome. Of course there have been yearnings and longings for release underlying our waking thoughts.

Two prisoners playing cards while a third prisoner sleeps.
Pencil drawing by **POW Mike Hardy, Changi POW Camp April 42**

I wonder how many times Deanna Durbin's rendering of "My Own" has wafted its way through these concrete buildings. Her performance is always welcomed even though it is less perfect now that both record and gramophone have felt the strain of constant use.

Every advantage has been taken of the talent that exists in a camp such as ours. A simply first rate play of A.A.Milne's "The Dover Road" has been played to packed audiences for two weeks, and it seems likely that it will run for some weeks to come. The standard of the acting is really high and even the female parts are most convincing in their 'femininity'. There is nothing amateur about these entertainments, and we have been amazed at the finish in dress and stage furnishings. Ingenuity has reached unbelievable heights. The facts are I suppose, that we have here behind the wire, men who comprise this civilian army whose everyday jobs are those which are now used in the multitudinous activities that make up this prison life.

Here and there in the camp are small plantations of rubber trees, they are not in production, but occasionally use is made of the white fluid which flows so freely from a gash in the bark. This raw rubber or latex as I understand it is called, can be mixed with a little petrol, and makes an excellent rubber solution, and has been used in the repair of rubber shoes and in numerous odd ways.

One is reminded of the value of skilled tradesmen in our ranks. Several lawn mowing machines have been converted and adapted to make rice mills. The rollers taken from these machines are fitted so that the rice is crushed. Some of these "Heath Robinson" machines are ambitious in design and most effective in operation. One I saw recently first crushed the rice, then through two oscillating pans, defective rice and weevils were eliminated and through further rollers the rice was ground to flour. I imagine about a third of our rice ration is now rendered into flour, and in this way greater use and variety can be made of our basic food.

We have no motor transport, except one ambulance for emergency use, but from broken up cars and lorries, an enormous variety of trucks and carts have been constructed. All are fitted with steering gear and some have four-wheel brakes and 'balbon' tyres.

We are lucky enough to have several sports fields, and so hockey and soccer are played throughout the evenings, and cricket too has many supporters. Less popular but very enterprising is the nine-hole golf course constructed by Divisional Signals. This is complete with a small bamboo Club House, built on lines similar to a Chinese temple.

Indoor games too have their devotees, bridge, or course, is frequently played. Other people have produced beautifully carved chess-men. I have often seen a crowd playing Monopoly, also home-made, and it is very good fun to watch the many games in progress in odd corners night by night. A certain number of periodicals and magazines have appeared, but the publication of these is cramped by the acute shortage of paper. From time to time though, an illustrated magazine will find its way into the mess. The contents always make good reading, and the poems are usually reminders of home and all that that means.

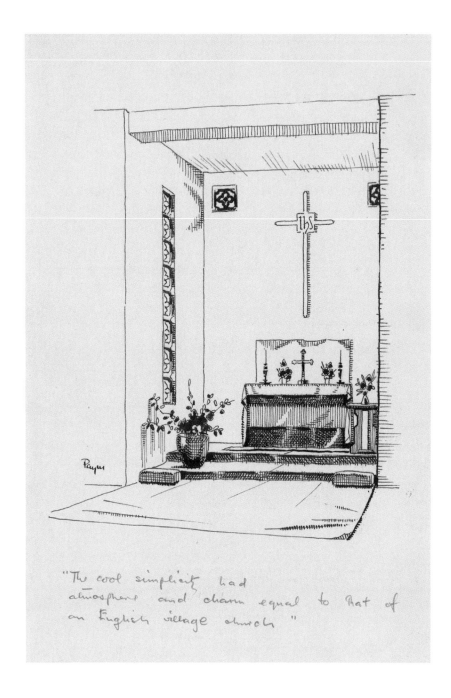

Pen and ink sketch by POW Payne of St George's Altar. On it he has written
"The cool simplicity had atmosphere and charm equal to that of an English village church."

A VISIT FROM THE BISHOP

A day of bitter disappointment was preceded by weeks of strenuous efforts to get things ready for the proposed visit of the Bishop of Singapore[*] for Confirmation. We had been told that he would endeavour to get to our camp in a fortnight's time. This naturally meant feverish activity on the part of the few padres left to muster their remaining candidates. During these past weeks my own number of candidates prepared for Confirmation had reached over one hundred and twenty.

The service was planned to be held in St. George's and we were in great excitement at the privilege of being the 'cathedral' for this unique occasion, Nearly two hundred candidates were to be present from our own Division, and from the other areas in the camp including the Australian lines[+].

Sketch of the new wooden pulpit made for St George's. It took a corporal and six men just a week to build it. Eric was very appreciative "The wood is tough, the tools are few and in this heat any manual work is a real effort. Theirs was a wonderful job".
By POW "L.K." 30.12.42

The Sapper officer who had designed our new Altar Rails produced sketches and plans for a new eight foot cross to replace the plain one above the Altar. A dignified design in contrasting woods both light and dark with a carved monogram IHS in the centre was chosen. Then a pulpit, and this piece of Church furniture met with much discussion and planning, sizes and shapes as well as designs were drawn, and finally we selected one that was in keeping with the modern design of the Altar Rails. I wish I were able to describe the technical details, which go with the building of such an ambitious thing as a pulpit. A corporal and six men were put on this our largest construction in the Church. They had just one week to complete it, and never have I seen men work so hard or so well as this team of craftsmen. The wood was tough, and hard to work, tools were few, and a supply of suitable wood hard to come by. Let it suffice that this fine team worked right through Saturday and most of Sunday in order to have their contribution ready for the proposed visit.

* Leonard Wilson (1897-1970) was the Bishop of Singapore from 1941-49. In 1943 he was held and tortured at Changi Prison.
+ Garrison Area

In this heat any manual work is a real effort, and theirs was a wonderful job. I need hardly add that half of that team were hoping to be confirmed, and several of the others regular communicants. But this does not complete our preparations, a new Credence table had been designed, and another carpenter was working on this, another was busy on a Processional Cross, on which he was putting a Figure which had been taken from a cheap Crucifix. Not to be outdone the Gunners promised to make two Churchwardens' staves, one surmounted with a carved crown, and the other with a mitre, symbolising Church and State, and more simply padre's and people's Warden.

As the day approached our activities increased, the choir had met for more practices. A special tea for guests was arranged, invitations were given to the Army Commander and the Generals commanding the various formations, Brigadiers, and Colonels too were among our honoured guests. Seating was collected for five hundred candidates and friends. Parties working outside the wire brought in armsful of brilliantly coloured flowers. The Altar and Chancel was a mass of these exotic blooms, and looked really beautiful. Boot polish and elbow grease made everything shine in Church. Service sheets were typed, and by noon of the day of the visit everything was in readiness, even to the finely made hassocks which were placed in front of the borrowed carved chair which stood impressively in the Chancel.

Soon after lunch candidates and friends began to arrive from the many parts of the camp. Officers were acting as ushers for the principle guests, and a group of sergeants offered to be sidesmen to shepherd people into their allotted seats. It was an impressive sight for one and all realised that this would be a day unique in our life and in the lives of prisoners of war. The candidates were keyed up, the early celebration that morning had been packed with them, for most of them have been regular communicants for weeks or perhaps months.

About ten padres including the senior chaplains were present, and we were all anxious and wondered if the Bishop would come. We realised that only recently he had been released from internment, and allowed a restricted amount of movement within his diocese by the Japanese. There were so many things which might hinder his coming. After sometime it seemed evident that he was delayed, and finally saddened and disappointed, the senior padre and myself conducted a short service and dismissed the candidates. Had this story ended here it would have been disappointing, but at the same time very well worth while, as it brought us all together in one big act of witness. But the story has a happy ending.

A day or so later we were informed officially that the Bishop would arrive for Confirmation in three days time. It was a marvellous surprise, and the news seemed definite, and so all the arrangements were again put into operation. It was easy because we had only to regard the previous gathering as a sort of 'dress rehearsal'. Again the stage was set, everything was as before, and at half past two a car drew up at the Church, and out stepped the Bishop in purple cassock and accompanied by an Indian Canon from the Cathedral, and a Japanese Officer who was an Anglican Christian. The Bishop had brought with him a small quantity of Bibles and Altar wine and wafers. As I was to be his Chaplain I busied myself with preparing his robes and assembling his Crozier. In a few minutes the procession was in place outside my room. First the Cross-bearer, then the choir of twenty-five officers and men, followed by the padres in their robes, and the two Churchwardens with their staves of office and last the Bishop and his chaplain. Leaving the verandah we proceeded along the road and entered this one-time mosque where five hundred voices were singing "We love the place O God". Present were the senior officers supplemented by a Dutch Army Commander and a member of his staff, and the little Japanese officer.

Standing in the pulpit the Bishop, having been given special permission to preach, talked to the candidates and gave them an inspiring message. He impressed us all and looked like a Bishop. He was a dignified figure in scarlet and white against the drabness of our khaki drill. And so in pairs the candidates knelt before the Bishop, officers, warrant officers, N.C.O.s and men. Some lame, others armless, many maimed in battle. One and all looking as smart as was possible in their much worn clothes.

Pen and ink drawing by POW of an amputee prisoner. In Changi there was an orthopaedic workshop where the prisoners made crutches and artificial limbs out of wood and leather and any other material they could scrounge.

After the service the Japanese officer gave permission to the Bishop to prolong his visit a little longer, so immediately we prepared for an Ordination Service. One of the Chaplains had been ordained Deacon in Singapore cathedral during the battle, and now he was to be ordained priest. He was a padre in the hospital, and priest's orders was essential in his work. The Altar was prepared for Holy Communion, and after the Bishop had met the various people who were anxious to talk to him, the padres preceded the Bishop into Church for this service. The various declarations and oaths of loyalty were made in my room.

So began the time honoured service from the Ordinal of our Prayer Book. After the reading of the Gospel there followed the reading of the exhortation and the questioning of the candidate, then the solemn laying-on of hands. The priests present grouped round the Bishop laid their hands too on this newly ordained priest. Then on to the prayer of Consecration, and the Communion of the Bishop and candidate and a few of those present, among them was the Japanese officer.

Probably for the first time in the history of Christendom a Confirmation and Ordination have been held in a mosque. Without precedent too must be the visit of an English Bishop into a prisoner of war camp in enemy occupied country, and historic and truly Christian was the presence of a captain in the Japanese cavalry. He knelt side by side with his enemies, next to him at the Altar Rails was an Indian, a few paces away between British tommies and officers was a Jamaican. Those who are still not convinced that Christianity is the one hope of the world, might do well to meditate on these things. If this can happen in the midst of a gigantic war, how much more can it influence and guide and direct nations in peace.

* * * *

It came about on the six months' anniversary of our captivity that all the senior officers were ordered to prepare to leave for Japan. Every officer above the rank of Lieut. Colonel was affected by this order, every "red tab" would be removed, and this meant officers of the Navy and R.A.F. as well as our own. Our division has suffered a great personal loss in our much loved and respected General and his Brigadiers. Other parties have been warned for Japan, and we have been told that they will be well looked after, and we in Singapore cannot expect a great amount of attention as we are living in what must even now be regarded as a battle zone.

Just after our commanders had left us the first supplies from the outside world reached us. A shipload of food from the Red Cross in South Africa was delivered into the camp. An excellent brand of dried soup, a pound of jam for each person and a handful of sweets, not ordinary ones but special vitamin filled caramels. Maize flour rich in Vitamin B completed this gift. It was appreciated tremendously, and was, we hope, the forerunner of other supplies.

One would have imagined that enough religion was emanating from St. George's throughout the day; the reader will have noticed that the facts of Christianity are finding their way into the lives of the prisoners. Yet another innovation has been introduced. I was asked to "put on" a mid-week service "quite short and simple nothing elaborate, something like the wireless service Mr. Elliott has at St.Michael's Chester Square". I should not presume to attempt an imitation of Mr. Elliott's famous talks, but I could model the service on his.

On Wednesday evenings at nine o'clock the flood-lights are switched on and the Church is packed from end to end for a twenty minute service. The Church looked most attractive and appealing, the lights piercing the blackness of the night, the intimacy of the lighting effect stopped many passers-by who, too, seemed attracted by this service.

A hymn sung seated followed by a lesson, and then in the darkness with just the glow from the pulpit light, a two or three minute address is given. One could feel in the darkness the intense atmosphere and the rapt attention of those present. The pulpit light is then switched off and the small floodlight turned on to the Altar, and in silence for five minutes the individual thoughts of those hundred or so men are focussed on their own prayers. A very real and thrilling little service which finished with the Blessing and so there has been established yet another link with home, another experience of real religion, a further deepening of the faith which so many have found and fostered in a life in captivity.

* * * *

The common cold which plagues the domestic life of the Englishman at home has its counterpart in this equatorial climate. Sufferers from it get as little sympathy in their suffering as the person in the throes of a detestable cold. The common complaint of this camp is a fever called dengue and is due to the bite of an infected mosquito. The symptoms are a high temperature and a chronic aching of the limbs, for this reason I suppose it is often called "break-bone" fever. One feels as if a horde of elephants has trampled over the body. The mediaeval tortures of the rack may be compared favourably with the unpleasantnesses of the dengue patient. After a week of erratic temperatures, one is left limp and dangerously depressed. A truly foul complaint, but such a common one.

HARVEST FESTIVAL

With our thoughts so often veering homewards we determined to keep our Harvest Thanksgiving services at a time when those time-honoured celebrations would be taking place at home. I announced that the last Sunday in September should be set aside, and appealed for flowers and gifts of fruit and vegetables. I did not ask for quantities, this would not be possible, but I was surprised beyond my wildest hopes. It was useless to attempt to decorate until the cool of Saturday evening, and then there was no dearth of helpers. During the afternoon baskets of vegetables arrived at regular intervals, soon my room resembled an oriental fruit stall. Sweet potatoes, purplish-green egg plant, those odd-looking "ladies fingers", tapioca root in its twisted and distorted shapes, kangkong and other bundles of green leaf vegetable was in evidence. Numbers of palm branches had been cut and were then fastened against the pillars of the Church. Tremendous bundles of brilliant hued flowers were left shyly at the entrance of the Church by the giver. The gift of flowers had meant a journey with a fatigue party outside the wire. The amount of flowers growing within the limits of the camp is very small.

As I received some of the gifts I felt deeply conscious of the sacrifice entailed, a handful of bananas or perhaps a cocoanut, either gift costing a few cents, but if your sole pay is nine cents a day this makes a real hole in it.

As the sun set the Church seemed to fill with that typical smell that fills our Churches at home at Harvest. Here I think the aroma from the frangipania or temple flowers overshadows the other more earthy smells. Someone had made a huge cross entirely of those pure white blooms, over a thousand of them went to make up this symbol of Christianity.

The pulpit too was decorated with the fernlike branches of the flamboyant tree or as it is also aptly named "flame of the forest". At the foot of the pulpit resting on a stand was a loaf modelled in the shape of a sheaf of corn, its weight was over 30 pounds. Pumpkins and gourds lined the sanctuary whilst the only decoration on the Altar was that of flowers, the choicest and best.

The spirit in which the men had entered into these celebrations is shown by the fact that some rose well before dawn to replace faded flowers with fresh ones.

The services need not be described in detail, the enthusiasm was typical of that shown in decorating. The three Celebrations of Holy Communion were packed and the voluntary services of Mattins and Evensong were crowded over an hour before the time due for the service. A visiting R.A.F. padre preached in the morning and among those present was the acting divisional commander and the commanding officer of the Dysentery Wing at the Hospital. To him were we sending the gifts which decorated the Church. The harvest hymns were sung for we realised that as we were thanking God for the fruits of the earth over which we had toiled, our prayers too were thanksgivings for the Harvest at home.

The first page of Eric's handwritten sermon entitled
Approaching God, which he preached in Changi on 5.10.42

SERMON: APPROACHING GOD

preached in Changi Gaol on 5th October 1942

"Let us have Grace whereby we may serve God acceptably with reverence and Godly fear" Mat.6.8.

"Your Father knoweth what things ye have need of, before you ask Him".

One of the things which each person has done during these last months - is a big chunk of <u>thinking</u>. During the long hot hours after dark, when you have had enough of conversation and argument – you have drifted off quietly – then you have run over in your mind all sorts of things. All sorts of things – the unfairness of human nature – the inequalities of life – the cushiness of some people's jobs – the way that some people always seem to fall onto their feet.

I've done that too, though only when depressed which doesn't often happen.

Probably at other times you have pondered on life and your particular lot – if you have been fair in your analysis or diagnosis – you will have found in your own bit of life quite a lot of good – a real amount of things to be cheerful over.

One of the things that many of you have come to grips with concerns God. It sometimes takes an upheaval – a strangeness such as this to jolt us and bring us face to face with the simple stuff of life. God belongs to the simple stuff – You have probably found it in many different ways but, summed up, it comes to – 'What is my relationship to God' – 'How if at all can God influence my life?' – In what way can God become real to me?' 'Can God possibly be concerned with the doings of one insignificant prisoner of war dumped on the blistering equator, God must be grappling with bigger problems than my fiddling little me?'

However the question is put, it all boils down to the God and Me Relationship. We have all attempted to get straight our ideas on God's place in life.

I want to give you just 2 ideas which, as I've pondered on that problem, have seemed so real. You don't want conventional phrases – you don't want a God decked up in attributes of fine phrases, which, when pricked, burst like bubbles.

What can we say of my relationship with my God?

And so the 1st point – let's start with me, that's you of course. I'm in your shoes for the moment. A man, not too fit, not too content gazing at his world. His mind still fresh with the experiences of war and prison and of travel and of peoples of all races and colours and creeds and languages. His mind grasping at the bigness of his world and feeling the smallness and insignificance of his place in the patterned mosaic of his world. This world of his, as his mind buzzes on, is so tiny in the face of the world he doesn't know. At night wandering thro the area of his prison camp he sees the worlds in the heavens as stars in the sky – he stops in his stride – so God is behind all this – the Power – the Force – the mind responsible for the universe. Either he feels it as some gigantic nightmare – or, rightly I think, - he feels humble – a sort of sense of awe and reverence – 'I am one of this God's created beings – one of His creatures.

Men of all time, in all ages high and low have felt rather like this about God – They bow the knee – in 'reverence and Godly fear' – in humility they kneel in the presence of their God. That was the first point – man's searching after God – man's approaches to God – his gropings after, his attempts to find God.

Then the 2nd point – here it is the other way round – just God's approach to man. God's attempt to get to know and be known by man. God has struggled to get through the selfishness and smallness of man's spoilt nature from earliest times. First in the ancient religions of the world – but superstition then has clouded out God, and the prophets in their time, but man turned a deaf ear.

So last of all – God ventured into the earth Himself clothed in the man Jesus Christ. From Him came the astounding news of a different relationship – at last God has managed to show His creatures the true relationship that must exist between Him and those made in His image.

The relationship is that of parent and child – father and son – God is as our father – to Him we are as children. That is the fact that blazes the trail thro the Gospels. That is the relationship that God, thro Jesus Christ has put across to man.

Do you see these 2 approaches in the eternal relationship of God and man? They are both so necessary – either one on its own is not complete – it gives a one-sided angle on God. The first - man's approach – a natural one of reverence and awe – and comes from our thought and efforts to place God into our scheme of living. The 2nd approach is the supernatural one of God's love for man and His desire from the beginning to establish a place in our thoughts and plans and prayers as a Father.

If human parents are concerned for the individual welfare of their children – God in all his might and power must make the best of human parents a poor, pale copy.

Well then, what real cause of worry or depression have I? You and I are of infinite value in God's eyes – that's all that matters, isn't it?

"A fellow could smoke a quiet pipe and be thankful"
Pen and ink drawing of Eric smoking a pipe in one of the pews in St George's *by POW Payne*

It is now a year since we sailed from England, it is difficult not to think too much of home and all it means, a prisoner of war has plenty of time for thinking. The anniversary was marked by large numbers at the early Celebrations.

* * * *

I am now quite expert at rolling my own cigarettes. I have bought some imitation Java loaf tobacco, we call it "Sikh's Beard", it is a definite improvement on the Malay variety in cigarettes which recently has contained more palm leaf than tobacco. There are no cigarette papers, but a good use has been made of air-mail paper. I find this admirable and in the last two days have smoked three sheets of first quality blue paper. I wonder if the writing pad will last our captivity? I would not have thought it possible to smoke a block of writing paper, I must consider a testimonial to the paper manufacturers … "I have smoked your writing paper for the past three weeks and find it in every way satisfactory" !

The greatest blow to the flourishing life centred round St. George's is the I.J.A. order to remove from this camp four-fifths of its number and transport them onto the mainland in the course of the next week. Our numbers will be reduced to a few hundreds, and we shall exist as a sort of staging camp. A party of Battalion strength has left each day and will continue to do so until there is left only the hospital and the men necessary for the maintenance of the camp and of course the many 'unfits'. This I am overjoyed to say does not mean the end of St. George's, it means that ours is now the only Church in our camp, and that we shall take over wider areas, it seems that there will still be the best part of two thousand to look after.

During the past two months many men have returned to Changi from the working parties in the town of Singapore because of unfitness. We are still ravaged by dysentery and more recently by diphtheria, and painful skin diseases. The latter are mainly due to deficiency in food. The irritation caused by these diseases has to be sampled to be believed, I speak with experience: ringworm or tinea is an unpleasant accompaniment to the other skin troubles. A minor nuisance, but a constant one is the ordinary bug, which seems to breed hourly and must owe its prolific reproduction to the nourishment received from the attacks on our persons, even sitting on hard wooden seats does not prevent the brutes from feeding lavishly.

Our life has its brighter side too. All officers are now paid the equivalent of about a pound a month and by using part of this to purchase supplies to supplement the hospital diet for the patients and to buy for the whole camp such articles of food that will help remedy deficiencies in the general diet. We purchase a kind of sun dried whitebait, evil-smelling but rich in vitamins, and red palm oil and rice polishings and other local produce such as towgay, which is a type of dried pea, and kangkong a green vegetable like spinach and full of nourishment.

Another high spot in our life has been the arrival of another Red Cross food ship. Foods too numerous to mention were on board and these have made a profound difference both to our diet and to the morale of us all, and we were issued too with sixty real cigarettes, called "Victory V", a significant gift we think.

During the past weeks parties of Dutch prisoners have arrived from Java and Sumatra, and we have enjoyed the comradeship of these visitors during their short stay before going up-country, and other parties continue to arrive.

St.George's has, I believe, helped our Dutch Allies. Large notices in Dutch and English were exhibited inviting them to Church, and so on Sundays now we have the lessons read in Dutch and English, as well as the Lord's Prayer and the Creed. It is most impressive to hear both National Anthems sung with such full-throated enthusiasm. Even the new choir which has been trained has several Dutch members.

New regulations demand a complete roll-call morning and evening. This evening parade has meant an alteration in the time of our "after-supper" activities, but the Church is now lighted from our local diesel engine, and so until halfpast ten each evening our talks, discussions and instructions and choir practices fill the Church.

One of the big things which must stand out as a milestone in our life is the Teaching Convention held each night for a week. The subject for the week was "What is the Church of England?" and the evening talks emphasised some vital aspect of our teaching and thought. It might be considered dull, but the evidence of those evenings showed a packed Church for the six consecutive meetings. Though the week coincided with the removal of those vast numbers up-country the crowded Church lost nothing in numbers. Men do want answers to questions that they themselves are ignorant of, and they want to be able to give an adequate answer to the constant barrack room discussion of religion. I have felt so much that even those most regular at Church know little of the traditions and teaching of our great Church. So it was that the fictitious Mr Oswald Twistle was a regular and popular figure featuring as the man with the grouse and the question, in the evening subjects. We tackled these time-honoured subjects: - "What is the C. of E?, Why the Prayer Book ? Why go to Church ? What is the Padre's job ? What Services are important ? and last What about you ?" We must attempt at home to teach our people even more than we have done in the past.

In the course of these notes I have made reference to our General who commanded our Division, a man known by us all and loved, to us he was "Becky". It was then a tremendous shock when we heard from the I.J.A. that he had died of diphtheria and heart failure in another prison camp overseas to which he and other senior officers were removed a month or so ago. To us it was a personal loss whose magnitude we cannot assess. Not only have we lost a man whose command we respected and whom to know was to love, but the Church on earth has lost a loyal and true son. He died on Armistice Day, and on the Sunday ten days later we, the remnants of the division, met for a memorial service. At Evensong in St. George's we paid to his memory that respect which we felt here as an intimate loss. He was an almost daily worshipper. May God rest his soul, he with 400 others have died in captivity, we remember them and those who will mourn them.

* * * *

Sometimes of an evening after supper and roll-call, it is good to wander away from the "daily round" and the constant chatter. Crossing the short sandy stretch outside my room leads one into the cocoanut groves where tents are dotted around. Another hundred paces and one is past all signs of one's fellows, here the ground slopes gently into what becomes in a few minute's walk a mangrove swamp. Wandering quietly through the coarse grass and seeking out the tracks on high ground it is rather wonderful to realise one's isolation. The deep-throated croak of the bull frog and the harsh though not unpleasant scrape of the cricket is the accompaniment to one's thoughts. How different is all this from the evening twilight of a stroll through those Cotswold hills. Here surrounded by wire yet free to wander over many hundred acres of this marshlike land one can feel and sometimes does feel lonely. Lonely in spite of the knowledge that two or three minutes away the hum and buzz, the singing and the lectures, the arguments and the games of hundreds of one's fellow prisoners mark the end of yet another day in a prisoner's life.

* * * *

Pencil drawing showing Changi Camp barracks and the onion dome of St George's, and, beyond them, mangrove swamps and the sea. *By POW C.B.Lee May 42*

ST NICHOLAS' DAY

I suppose to those who might be ignorant of the date, the presence of Santa Claus in Church on December 6th would seem odd. A tall red-cloaked figure with the traditional white beard, but on his head a fine red mitre, and in his hand a truly episcopal crozier. Santa Claus was dressed as he should be, as a Bishop and a Saint of the Church, who was no figment of the imagination but a real person of fifteen hundred years ago. It appears that in Holland and in the Netherland Indies St. Nicholas' Day is a great Festival of the children, a time for fun and games, and the giving and receiving of presents, whilst Christmas Day is observed as a Church festival only. The Dutch troops in camp decided that Saint Nicholas should visit us, so he was chosen from one of their number and dressed in his traditional costume. Then enthroned on one of the camp trucks, converted from old motor lorries, and escorted by three native servants, in this case real coloured men, he toured the camp. A programme of sports and games had been arranged, and as December 6th was a Sunday, I suggested that Santa Claus and the Dutch and British should first come to Church. We had a short and simple service in both languages and our thoughts and prayers were for our children, and children everywhere.

* * * *

Prisoner dressed up as a jaunty St Nicholas enthroned on one of the camp trucks during a tropical rainfall. This was to celebrate St Nicholas' Day December 6th 42. *Pencil drawing by POW "LK"*

It has not been necessary to write of the seamy side of a prisoner's life, because for the vast majority life is full of activities of all sorts, work and play has ensured a healthy mentality, but it is to be expected that there are those who by their selfishness and greed cause unpleasantness. The man who is willing to organise a "black market", and so make money by selling at a great profit goods he has acquired, he is a blight on our community life, and so is the petty thief. During Sunday Evensong recently one of those light-fingered folk removed from my room such spare clothes as I possessed, with oddments of money and toilet articles. This form of crime is felt more keenly here as it is impossible to replace by purchase any articles stolen. Again, though, one is overwhelmed by the comradeship that exists, and within a few days I had been showered with gifts from officers and men, who were anxious to share such articles as they possessed. This generosity is something which has made me feel the privilege of serving amongst men who are so fundamentally grand and big.

How large in one's life loom these petty incidents, incidents that rattle and annoy, and assume such formidable proportions. There had been a spate of this thieving during the early weeks of our captivity. Stolen from my room was the bread for Holy Communion and two pipes and what remained of a tin of tobacco. My rage was such that over the tornado that served as a sermon at Evensong on that Sunday, I am still leg-pulled.

* * * *

CHRISTMAS

On Christmas Eve the moon made the whole landscape of tall clustered palms and squat huts swim in a warm light. That moon is not the pale thing of the north but is as masterful as the sun itself. Below the dome of St. George's the atap-roofed verandahs twinkled with hanging lamps made from half shells of cocoanuts and inside a bully beef tin filled with palm oil and having a floating wick. Then nearer still at the entrance stood a Christmas tree, a local imitation of our English fir reaching to the roof. Reflecting the lights from little lamps fastened to the branches were stars, small horse-shoes, all shapes and sizes of tinfoil covered objects. Then inside the church itself, the pillars

Christmas Eve in St George's.
"The chancel was a mass of candlelight and the feathery green ferns enhanced the setting." *Sketch by POW "L.K."*

were covered with ferns, and along the low wall between the arches stood pots of coloured flowers. Both Dutch and British troops went out with trucks to collect all these decorations. But one's gaze was centred on the chancel, here in a mass of candle light, the Altar was emphasised as the focal point. A row of candles were fastened above the Altar, and three-branched tall candlesticks stood on either side; the flowers and feathery green ferns enhanced the setting for the Celebration of Holy Communion that was to take place at midnight.

But our Christmas festivities were preceded by vast preparations which must first be recorded. First perhaps was the application to the I.J.A. for permission to hold a midnight service after lights-out. Oddly enough the petition was put forward on behalf of St. George's and when granted was enthusiastically taken up by the R.C.s , for their Midnight Mass and by the Free Church and the Salvationists for services to be held at this hour.

Then someone had the brainwave and grand idea of making toys for the sixty British children in the civilian jail which is situated just outside the perimeter wire of our camp. A week before Christmas an exhibition of toys was arranged; to visit it was to recapture the scene of the toy department of any large London store. It was thrilling, scooters, engines, prams, rocking horses, and smaller toys such as dolls and whipping tops, they were all beautifully made and finished. The rapt expression on men's faces as they lingered over this display, was a foretaste of the thrill that those kiddies must have had in receiving each four or five of these toys. The Japanese authorities gave permission for these toys to be sent to the jail, and a touching letter of thanks was received from the women's representative in the prison. It would have been marvellous to have been present, though it is not difficult to picture that scene. It must have done much to brighten the life of those little children who, for various reasons, could not be evacuated before the capitulation.

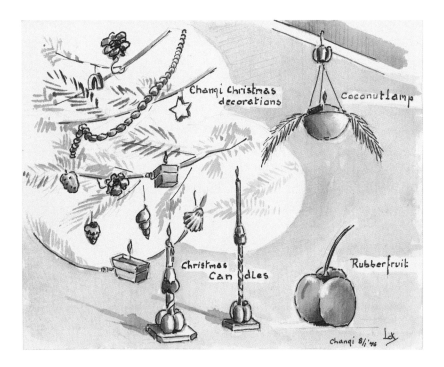

Christmas decorations made from shells and fruit and tinfoil wrapped stars. The POWs also made toys for the 60 British children imprisoned in the civilian jail outside their camp. They made scooters, engines, prams, rocking horses and dolls and whipping tops, all beautifully finished so that the collection looked like the toy department of any large London store.
Pen and ink drawing by POW "LK" December 42

On Christmas Eve on the padang, a two acre green patch almost opposite the Church, was erected a stage with electric lights shining down from poles fastened to the corners of the platform. Behind this, in curved rows was a massed choir of a hundred and the theatre orchestra. It was around this platform that at half past eight three thousand men were grouped for a concert of carols. After the singing of a carol, a solo artist would entertain that crowd by a song, piano playing, or perhaps a fiddle solo. The standard of these performers was not amateur, for we have here many first rate professional musicians. From the platform the impression I received was that of a vast sea of faces, and so the familiar carols went up in a mighty roar. The programme reached its climax in a short service and a Dutch ceremony of the kindling of the light. After the reading of the Christmas story from the Gospels, a large bowl on a stand was placed on the platform and then stepped forward a Dutch Naval Officer, and speaking into an imitation microphone gave an imaginary broadcast to our families scattered across the seas. He painted the scene and in a moving speech depicted the blackness of our present life, a life not relieved by the bright distracting lights of pre-war living. He told of the black hour of the Dutch folk living as they were in countries under the heel of the enemy. Then presently three men, an officer, a N.C.O. and a soldier poured oil into the bowl, then lighting this with a torch, he spoke of the light of the Christmas message, the coming of Light into the world and into our hearts – a light which shines so brightly now because of the blackness that at present surrounds the world. It was all very impressive. I gave in English a short précis of the ceremony and then said some prayers and gave the Blessing, and so began our celebration of our first Christmas as prisoners.

Half an hour later the Church was packed for the midnight Eucharist. Eight hundred men were grouped in and around the little ex-mosque, and so began the first Celebration of that service which is the central act of worship of Christians throughout the world. A carol then the plaintive melody of Merbecke's music accompanied the service of our Prayer Book liturgy. Present in Church were the senior officers of the Division and representatives of the Dutch Forces. Just after midnight in an atmosphere that was real and moving those familiar words "O come let us adore Him" quietly hushed and rising as a prayer were sung after the final words of the Prayer of Consecration had been said. To us indeed the "Word was made flesh and dwelt among us and we beheld His glory, the glory as of the only-begotten of the Father". The Altar rails filled and emptied as four hundred men in turn knelt and received his Communion. The shabby green uniform of the Dutch Army was emphasised in these rows of kneeling khaki clad figures. Present too were those maimed in battle, an empty sleeve, a stump of leg. Outside the moon was reflected on the shiny surface of the palm branches, and in the ear vibrated the persistent hum of the crickets. Streaming back to their billets were men who had recaptured a glimpse of our Christian Christmas, an experience not easily forgotten. Peace on earth to men of goodwill, that was the prayer in each person's mind, as was the thought for our homes which are the successors of that first little Family, simple prayers but so real.

The next Celebration began in the dark at half past seven on Christmas morning, and the chancel with its many candles reflected light sufficient until the coming of the dawn, and so followed another service and then breakfast. During the meal the orchestra grouped on the centre of the padang played carols. Our meals throughout the day were most attractive. For the first time we were able to drink coffee with tinned milk, a luxury, and breakfast was made more exciting by some fish fried with chipped potatoes. A Sung Eucharist followed by a Carol Service completed the services for the day. In the evening we ate a most superior dinner. Ten scraggy cockerels carefully nursed for months provided the 'plat du jour', preceded by soup and followed by a fair imitation of plum pudding. It was the right colour and had dates in it. We drank a home brewed pineapple cyder, though the word 'cyder' makes it sound more potent than it really was, but in the hackneyed words of those local newspaper reports – "a good time was had by all". A gigantic concert on the padang filled the evening and at eleven o'clock we joined the Dutch Officers for some supper. A subscription to the value of tenpence was raised, and in a mess room decorated with paper tablecloths, and lit by little lamps seventy officers were seated round a horseshoe shaped table. A three-course meal began with a thick soup, a speciality of Java, then a sardine sandwich. This was the first slice of bread tasted for many months, for the supply of flour was exhausted some time ago. The sweet may best be described as a sweet soup, a favourite from the East Indies, called Kolak, which was rich and sweet and pleasant and seemed to contain pineapple and cocoanut juice. Speeches and toasts were made and the day was rounded off with coffee sometime in the small hours.

Two days later on the Sunday evening St. George's was the scene of the Nine Lesson Carol Service, so familiar to radio listeners at home. The carols which had been carefully rehearsed were interspersed with nine short readings from the Bible. Each lesson is read by a representative of the life of the particular community. Lessons here were read by a Colonel, a Major, a Captain, a Sergeant-Major, a Corporal and a Private, and also a Dutch Naval Officer and a soldier of the Dutch army. These represented the Dutch forces, our camp, the Gunners, the Sappers, the Fusiliers, the R.A.S.C., and R.A.O.C., and the infantry. It was good to hear the lessons read in the dialects with which we are so familiar in England.

I was surprised but thrilled that so many made a real effort to prepare for Christmas by asking that their confessions might be heard. It was more than the usual few instructed folk to whom this was their custom. Quite a few men, even including Dutch, came to me in Church for this purpose before the festival. I feel I can look back on those days as a definite milestone in my life.

PERSONALITIES

I am reminded in these disjointed paragraphs that unwittingly I may have left the impression that life is fairly grim and heavy and even rather "ecclesiastical", that obviously would not be a true picture. There are many light moments, and as the months have passed a sense of humour has done much to keep our life healthy. I have refrained from the mention of personalities except in the vaguest of terms, because I have felt that a mass of names would bewilder and confuse the reader. Yet of course one's whole life is linked with persons, I would then for a moment or two put right this omission by writing of some of one's daily companions. There have been several of one's fellow padres, Fred, and David, the "little priest", the S.C.F., the A.C.G. whose help and friendship have been so valued. The "Doc" has been mentioned before, we have been soldiering (an inapt term applied to us!) for three years and we have fought together in all senses of the word. He has a delightful sense of humour and when his punning is not too puerile is very witty. Without knowing it he often restores my sense of proportion by some such remark – "I have tried to fix an appointment to see the padre in his room, but he can only offer me 2.30 next Thursday when I am to be sandwiched between a Brigadier and a Colonel" . Again he will say in a tired voice – "This morning I had 25 Baptisms, 41 Confirmations and five funerals", a friendly dig at my love of counting heads.

One would expect many rows and disagreements but it is amazing how little there is, which is the more remarkable in view of our "enclosed" existence. Then there is "Titus" who is a prolific talker and an enormous eater, he invariably clears up eagerly any "left-overs" on the table, even to the evil-smelling whitebait. It is a joy to see the light in his eyes when a large "lump of duff" (a correct description of it) is placed in front of him, still he turns the scale at fourteen stone in peace time. He is my new sacristan. Like all here I lost so many friends in the exodus up-country, including Peter, a major and an ordinand, a pre-war stockbroker, but too a lover of country pursuits, I miss him very much. Then there is Wilky who shares our table of Fusilier Officers and we have served together from the time of going to France. He used to be called "fat Wilky", but now he is a mass of skin and bone. He is my Churchwarden and helped so much in getting St. George's started. Jack, Willie and J.B. went up-country too, grand fellows, Fusilier Officers, and they were Servers as well as mainstays of the choir. There is Bill of the R.A.S.C. of "Borehole Bugle" fame. The Borehole Bugle is the name given to his daily announcements of rumours and what we call "bore-holes", which is highly coloured and very doubtful items of the war. John and Eric are Sapper officers, who together have designed , and are at present planning vast improvements in our Church furnishings, but more of that in due course. Adrian and "Simmie" complete our table of six with Wilky, the "Doc" and Titus. Adrian so often resembles a Buddha in his favourite posture of almost complete nudity, while puffing a pipe which seems to contain a ripe assortment of garbage. Personalities there are in plenty. Reginald[*], is now my organist and choir-master, two previous organists have left the camp. Reginald is probably one of England's leading pianists, he is a brilliant musician and a droll lecturer in all branches of music. He is a private in the Army and contrives quite unconsciously to look the complete professor of music. Long hair and a certain untidiness of person, and on his feet a pair of enormous army boots with no socks. He is one of the most charming persons I am privileged to have as a friend, he has a faith that really matters too. I would like to write of Sandy and John Willie, and the many one has learnt to know in a way that before was not possible.

---

[*] Reginald Renison died in September 1943 on the Burma Railway. He was 35 years old.

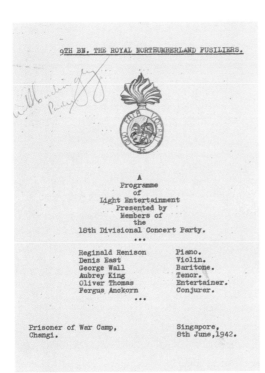

I began this paragraph by writing of lighter things and before mentioning incidents which have amused us tremendously I would add that half a dozen and more concert parties tour several openair stages. They are reminiscent of the seaside show on the pier, one is aptly named the "Kokonut Grove". These shows are enormously popular.

1.	PIANOFORTE SOLOS.		
	Valse	... ...	Chopin.
	Two Studies	... ...	Chopin.

2.	TENOR SOLOS.	
	I'll sing thee songs of Araby...	Clay.
	You are my heart's delight ...	Lehar.
	O Sole Mio	Ed. di. Capud.

3. IMPERSONATIONS.

" The March of Time."

4.	VIOLIN SOLOS.		
	Zigeunerweisen ...	...	Sarasate.
	Serenade Espagnol ...	...	Charminade.

5. "WIZARDUS"

"An Exhibition of Magic"

6.	BARITONE SOLOS.		
	Fishermen of England	Sanderson.
	Fill a Glass with Golden Wine ..	Quilter.

7.	PIANOFORTE SOLOS.		
	Moment Musical	... ...	Schubert.
	Liebestraume	... ...	Lizt.

8. MONOLOGUE.

" Ode to Rice "

9.	TENOR SOLOS.	
	Ah, I here sighed to rest me (Il Travstore)..	Verdi
	A Wandering Minstrel (Mikado)	Sullivan.

10.	VIOLIN SOLOS.		
	Caprice Viennois ...	...	Fritz Kreisler.
	Serenade (Student Prince) ...		Romberg.

11. MORE MAGIC !

12.	BARITONE SOLOS.		
	To Mary	... ...	N.B.White.
	Toreador Song	... ...	Bizet.

--- THE KING ---

Typed programme for an evening's Concert Party given by prisoners on 8 June 42.
Reginald Renison, one of London's leading pianists,
was organist and choirmaster at St George's.

Prisoners struggling to move a truck loaded with equipment.
The POWs took advantage of trips outside the camp to 'acquire' badly needed supplies.
Drawing by POW Payne 1942

The first incident which we chuckle over concerned a party of prisoners in the town who were engaged in road repairs, and who each morning solemnly visited the Jap authorities to procure a four gallon tin of petrol, a closely rationed fluid. It did not seem to surprise anyone that this liberal supply was collected on behalf of a steam roller. The contents of this tin yielded many dollars when sold to discriminating Chinese.

Another yarn arose from the inspection by the I.J.A. for a number of tins of stolen tobacco. The Nippon soldiers must have been very simple souls because in their very thorough search they came upon a promising-looking box which contained a concealed radio-set. *(the words ' radio-set' were left blank in the typed text and had been added in pencil, in Eric's writing, later)* An annoyed grunt from the investigator was the only remark on seeing this forbidden article. One can only presume that he was so intent on his lost smokes that his mind was unable to register this bigger find.

* * * *

In writing these pages I have made frantic efforts to divide the material into chapters. It became a nightmarish business. Months ago I drafted out ideas, they came so easily, The Battle, The Aftermath, The First Weeks, From Weeks to Months, then came the inevitable gloomy conclusion that From Months to Years would be the next chapter. Putting aside the depression arising from such thoughts, and inspired by reading some really excellent modern novels, I have come to the conclusion that if chapters have to be, they can probably be sorted out at the desk in that quiet study overlooking the Rectory garden.

Here I must digress and regret the fact that in the past years I have been missing some first rate literature in favour of the Penguin type of detective yarns, which until these past months have been my relaxation. A.G.Street, Ann Bridge, Ethel Boileau, Angela Thirkell, and a whole host of others, who are, I assume, household names to the reading public. These have been a thrilling tonic to a fit of gloom and a real link with England's countryside. Such copies of these and other authors' works have been so well handled, that our bookbinders have provided new covers and have stitched in pages time and again.

This preamble which is becoming dangerously longwinded is merely to herald a sound reason for a break in these pages.

SUMMARY

We have been a year behind this wire. I ought to attempt some sort of summary. Probably one of the most serious considerations at the present time is in the matter of food. We have fared reasonably well with the aid of the supplies from the Red Cross ship of some months ago, hunger and illness have been controlled. Those supplies are exhausted and for many weeks now meat even its previous minute quantity has been crossed off the menu. In its place fish, the fresh sort is issued. I presume it is fresh when it leaves its tropical waters, but after several miles of journeyings in an open truck, and a sorting out on an open barrack square, it needs a strong stomach, or stronger camouflage in flavouring matter to consume the stuff. It averages out at about half an ounce a day, which of course includes the head and bones and other unedible parts. The few other European oddments of food such as cocoa and flour are finished. The meals are then in the main rice and unsweetened milkless tea, the former is put on the table in the form of porridge, buns, pasties and tartlets, and happily our fresh vegetable ration is at present adequate so that sweet potatoes and pumpkin and other locally grown "green stuff" help a monotonous meal-time.

The medical authorities have advised us to eat an ounce or two of rice polishings daily. In appearance it resembles bran, and is used in ordinary times for pig feeding. A closer inspection reveals it to be a heaving mass of weevils, worms, and bits of still life such as grit and glass. In taste it has an unpleasant tang, as well as a clogging effect on the jaws. But it is consumed because of its redeeming virtue of a high content of this much prized vitamin B. I need make no further mention of the whitebait and other evil smelling native oddments that are purchased in the villages. We used to consider it odd to eat a mixture we called manure, in truth a fertiliser, which was the residue of ground nuts after the oil had been extracted, on retrospection that was quite a delicacy.

The routine of the day is almost invariable. It is odd how grateful one is for that element of routine. It gives form and substance to these dateless days. It seems to place on them a brand value, however faint, which somehow guarantees their worth. And these days are worthwhile. I can say that truthfully after one year's living of them. Certain of them stand out in importance, others are just ordinary yet strangely valuable.

Reveille sounds at eight o'clock, and as yet the sun has not risen, then a scramble to be on parade for roll-call a quarter of an hour later. This is a short business, and so back to prepare the Altar for the Celebration. But I have described in some detail a typical day, and the only alteration is the present evening roll-call. This is likely to be a lengthy affair depending on the whim and punctuality of our guards. We are numbered and checked and renumbered until with some display of dumb show everyone is satisfied. The odd command is given – "To the front, salute; down". The salute is taken with some dignity by the squat, untidy, little brown-faced senior soldier of the I.J.A. As I have previously intimated this compulsory parade has necessitated alteration in the daily routine of many months. There follow lectures both of a popular sort and of the university extention type. The Theological faculty has a lecture each Tuesday, which is as popular as the others, and for the time being must suffice for the Ordinands. Many of them went up-country, as well as my two experienced lecturers.

The Church flourishes again at the end of these evening lectures, when for an hour or until light-out I have planned special courses, discussion groups, debates, and Confirmation instruction. Since the reader is familiar with my apparent love of statistics, I may be allowed to record the year's total of two hundred Confirmation candidates. To me this will always be one of the big things of this prison life, because I know it means that number of keen, trained laymen. Then this year has seen over ten thousand Communicants at the Altar Rails of St.George's, and I cannot omit the reference to twenty-one men who have been baptised. So we begin the living out of a second year.

It would be wrong to assume that the enthusiasm for religion that has been such a big factor would gradually peter out as months of regular routine absorbed the novelty of the early days, especially as the memory of the grimness of battle faded.

I am convinced that an impartial observer would say that the life centred round the Church is maintained and indeed on the increase. My present class for Confirmation instruction is forty in number. Our congregation for Evensong on Sunday has doubled in the past six months.

Spiritually then, in as far as it is possible to assess, I believe we are in fair fettle. From a rough census of the barrack rooms and billets it appears that over sixty percent of the men here do regularly and voluntarily attend Church services each week. It is absolutely voluntary and I would say that a much bigger proportion go to Church from time to time.

Bodily we are not in such a flourishing condition. I have written of the various diseases, especially of the vitamin deficiency type. These diseases take a heavy toll of our numbers, thin emaciated bodies are attacked by skin complaints and tropical sores. The sun tan hardly hides the poor physical condition.

Then sartorially we are some degrees worse. From the Red Cross supplies of months ago we were equipped from head to foot, but not in the middle. Boots there were, and we were on our uppers, and the only other general issue was a hat. It was and still is a khaki edition of the familiar soft felt hat which is our usual headgear at home. It is most suitable as it is light and stands rain better than a topee, and it provides an effective shade from the sun. Militarily it probably gives the sergeant-major a headache because unlike the Field Service or forage cap, it is able to adapt itself to the character of the wearer. There is the jaunty "pork pie" style ("officially" forbidden), the man-about-town with brim up at the back and down at the front, or the country style with brim down at front and back. It adds a spice to roll-call to glance from the rows of faces to the hats above them. We present a ragged and drab appearance. Our faded shirts and shorts have had fifty washings, though that must be an over-statement to judge from some grubby figures.

Our tattered appearance belies the true spirit of the camp, morale is excellent. This is due, I believe, in the main to the fact that we have days well filled with work, and that there are several hundreds of acres to move about in. We are living in our peace and war formations. Batallions, often of skeleton strength, exist as units, with Officers, N.C.O.s, and other ranks. It is obvious that this has kept a sound atmosphere of discipline and routine, and so we have not become mere rabble. No man need be bored nor worsened by this enforced captivity.

Pencil drawing by POW Mike Hardy entitled "Grass Fatigue", he adds
"This person obviously cannot use a scythe"! Changi POW Camp 24.5.42

There is a garden next to the Church. Several keen gardeners have scoured the camp collecting plants and shrubs from the gardens of the peace time married quarters inside the wire. It is a colourful patch on either side of the stone flagged entrance. I do not know whether these flowers are representative of Malaya, but they are not to be compared with the sweet smelling herbaceous borders of England. The torrential rain followed by days of blistering sun tend, I suppose, to encourage a coarse and spindly growth. I proudly picked a coveted bunch of bananas from this garden to-day. From these tall plants with leaves as large as sacks grow an enormous purple bud, which unfolds each day to reveal a row of pale yellow flowers, from which the fruit develops. The bananas are picked green and earlier than is normal, due to the obvious fact that others covet this fruit, I could not stand the loss by "a thief in the night" of this handsome bunch. It is as pleasant to offer folk a banana or two as it is to heap the admiring visitor with asparagus cut from your own bed at home.

St George's Mark 1 in the POW Camp at Changi Feb 1942 – April 43. The little mosque was
converted into a church with new furnishings made by the prisoners. These include metal
candlesticks, a wooden pulpit, the brass cross and the plaque of St George and the Dragon.
Watercolour painting by Lieut. E Stacy RE 1943

I must now write of the alterations carried out in Church. To us it means so much because it is the centre of our life, and so many are engaged on the various jobs and also because the work has not been rushed or slipshod but has been the daily work of many of the Sappers for two months. Work which has been the best that the many craftsmen here could produce. I wish it were possible to convey the thrill which I get each day in wandering through the various workshops, and seeing the progress that has been made, and in delighting in the skill and workmanship that has gone into that progress. Seats for latrines, new handles for shovels are necessary jobs but how much more exciting it is to build to a given plan and design something which will make the Church more beautiful. As an illustration of what I mean, and anticipating the description that will follow, the new Altar is an example. This is to have riddell posts with curtains and dorsal, which is the technical description of an English Altar with four posts standing upright at each corner of the Altar, from which at the sides and back will hang curtains. Eric and John, the Church architects have planned that this should be carried out in wrought iron with decorated finials at the top of each post. Two or three blacksmiths and several fitters are working on this, but unfortunately the right sort of soft iron is not to be found on the metal dump, but only lengths of tool steel. In consequence the work on this type of iron has been almost superhuman, especially with such a lamentable shortage of tools. They have a few badly worn hacksaw blades, and after much hammering and forging, it may take a day to file a groove the thickness of a finger.

To return to the sequence of events, the first of the improvements was made in Church in rebuilding the Sanctuary steps on which the Altar is raised. The rough and ready platform has been planed and finished with an extra step. A strip of cocoanut matting was cunningly altered to the width of the Altar, and we have stained and wax-polished the steps on either side of the carpet. Next to be designed and made was a Lectern built on to a small dais, and the design is a variation of that used in the Altar Rails, the pulpit and credence table. One of the illustrations will give you the idea, and will indicate how well it is suited to the simple architecture of the building. Then there is the Priest's Stall and prayer desk which replaces one that has done so well and was made twelve months ago from shelves taken from a cupboard and built with the aid of a penknife. The new stall has the same fundamental design which to me defies description. There is a central panel on both the stall and desk carved with the badge of the Chaplain's Department. The size of a large plate, this panel has carved a Maltese cross surrounded by a wreath of oak leaves and surmounted by a crown.

Plaque of St George slaying the Dragon which is an elaboration of the badge of the Royal Northumberland Fusiliers. It was carved from wood and painted with oil paints, and took the prisoner, who was a sculptor, a month to complete. Eric was very upset when it was mislaid up-country in Thailand, but eventually he found some Japanese guards using it as a dart board and he reclaimed it for his church.

So we come to the Altar. Most striking of all is an octagonal plaque which is fastened by ornamental brackets, and is, in effect, a reredos, with a curtain behind it. This wooden plaque is carved in bas relief and depicts St. George slaying the dragon. The design is an elaboration of the badge of the Royal Northumberland Fusiliers and has taken a craftsman over a month to carve. He is by profession a sculptor, and this is his first venture in wood. It has been painted in oils and is probably one of the most lovely things yet made in the camp. In front of the blue side and back curtains the wrought iron work seems to be most fitting and dignified. Perhaps it is made the more beautiful against the white-washed wall and the Moorish style of the building. I cannot think why such materials are not used in England, but perhaps it has been used, it certainly deserves wider recommendation. How much lovelier and more dignified this is compared with the gaudiness and often tawdriness of the fittings in so many of the chancels of our parish Churches at home. We are perhaps a unique colony, having amongst us men who are skilled in all the arts, and here it is not commercialised and turned into work at so much an hour. It is because of such things as these, which tiny and unimportant as they probably are in themselves, that I have felt that an attempt to write of these things was necessary.

Many weeks had been allowed for the new work in the Church, but on the evening before the dedication, carpenters, painters, iron workers were clambering over each other putting the final touches to the Altar, even that excellent person, my batman, was busy with needle and cotton doing odd adjustments.

The Services on the Sunday of the anniversary were memorable, and the A.C.G. preached at the dedication in the morning. It seemed rather wonderful to think back over the past year; a year of change and progress, and certainly not of stagnation. I wish it were possible for the reader to feel the atmosphere of this life. To describe it is to make stilted and obvious remarks. Its reading reminds me of those Church accounts by a "cub" reporter on a country newspaper. These ordinary incidents seem somehow vital, they seem to possess some fresh quality which raises them above common routine.

HOSPITAL

The next day I was in hospital. To each of us the hospital has meant something, and to some it has meant much. For the first time I am able to see it as a patient. Feeling horribly bogus and a complete fraud, I have merely a sort of ringworm infected abscess on the face. I am surrounded with year old battle casualties, cheerful limbless limping men. I have a bed on the third storey verandah of a camouflaged concrete barrack block overlooking a silver strip of sea which separates this island from the mainland. Dense jungle and marsh land, a vivid green patch broken by muddy creeks, forms the foreground.

The first night was made hideous by the noises. The myth of the stillness of tropical nights needs "debunking". There is the pulsating hum of the cricket, with the harsh noises of insect life, but above all is the sleep-destroying croak of the frog. Like some Dante's conception of a gigantic maddened orchestra of trombonists condemned eternally to blast notes out of tune. A battery of motor horns could hardly produce a more discordant din. Perhaps a sleepless tossing about tends to exaggerate this nightly row which follows a day of rain. My first impressions were aggravated by a night of restlessness due in no small measure to the bed bug. This entirely loathsome creature had embedded itself in the hair mattress, I imagine that complete annihilation can only be effected with a blow lamp.

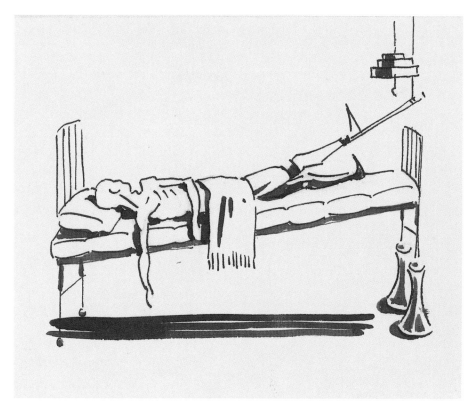

Hospital Patient. Eric wrote: "We are starving, not melodramatically, but slowly, scarcely a third of the camp is fit to work. The more serious are in hospital, a pitiful and grim picture they present." *Pen and ink sketch by POW, Changi.*

Here in our camp is a hospital of two thousand patients organised by our own staff of doctors and orderlies. Apart from water and electric light supplied by the I.J.A. it is merely a series of barrack blocks converted into a vast surgical and medical hospital. On the staff as a consultant is an eminent London surgeon, a prisoner of war, but doing a wonderful job under difficult conditions. There are many hundreds who owe their lives and limbs to the skill and devotion of this staff. Drugs and equipment are inadequate. To me this has been a wonderful fortnight. It has meant a change of atmosphere, and too, of diet. In hospital the Red Cross rations are still carefully eked out. In the past two months there has been no meat, just simply rice, and vegetables and scraps of fish. In hospital bully beef rissoles have been a grand attraction. These extras are thrilling after what is a starvation diet. We are starving, not melodramatically, but slowly, scarcely a third of the camp is fit enough for work, various appalling skin diseases are rife. The more serious are in hospital, a pitiful and grim picture they present, too loathsome to describe. There is though a cheerfulness in the camp. And one is not really conscious of our plight except in these odd realistic moments.

As I sit on my bed a symphony and choral concert in the Palladium, one of the camp theatres, is playing to an audience of five hundred. An orchestra of 25 players has just played a Schumann concerto, and now a male voice choir is singing "Comrades in Arms". Here has been produced an orchestra whose talent is first rate, and who somehow are able to overcome the poor quality of some of the instruments. I have mentioned the plays that have been staged, we have seen too, Sheriff's "Badger's Green", "I killed the Count", "Loyalties". These and others have been played by men who are professional actors, and produced by men of West End experience.

I have wondered so much if prisoners in other camps in other parts of the world have lived so fully a year as that which has been ours. Hardships there have been, I have tried to record that side, but that side has not, I am convinced, warped our lives, lives which in adversity has shown human beings to be made of such fine stuff. The future may be harder yet, still our philosophy is to live each day as fully as can be. Does this sound horribly trite, I hope not?

* * * *

end of typed diary

Living Skeletons
April 1943 – April 1944
Kanburi, Thailand on the Burma Railway
Eric Cordingly's secret notes and military report

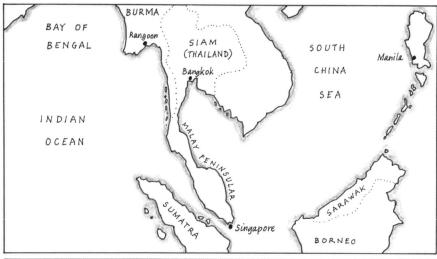

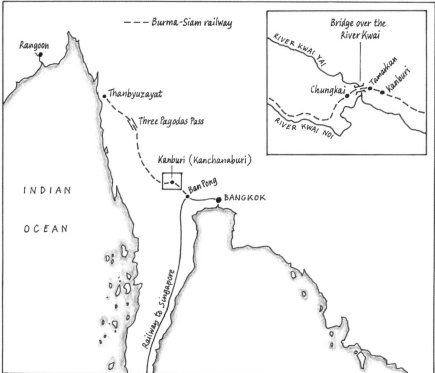

Maps of the Malay Peninsular in the 1940s. The POWs travelled from Singapore to the staging post at Ban Pong (Bampong) in iron trucks, a journey which lasted 5 days. The track of the Burma–Siam Railway on which they laboured is shown with a dotted line. Kanburi (Kanchanaburi) staging camp and Kanburi Hospital, where Eric Cordingly was based, were situated close to the River Kwai. *Drawn by David Cordingly*

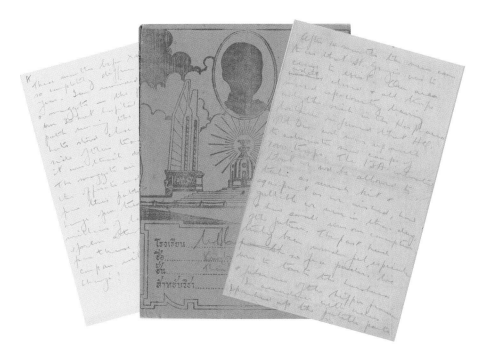

When Eric was sent up-country to Thailand, to the Burma Railway, he kept secret notes first
on airmail paper and then in a Thai child's exercise book.

TRAVELLING UP-COUNTRY

After 14 months the news came to us that St. George's was to cease to exist. Our area would be closed and all troops moved up-country leaving only the sick in the Hospital area. We were informed that HQ of the Division would move up north to administer the new camps of 7000 troops. The I.J.A. intimated that we would be allowed to take as much kit and equipment as we wished. How gullible we were in those days and how small was our conception of the future. The past had been truly wonderful, especially so for a padre. We were to taste the harshness and falseness of the Nippon promises. In accordance with orders I packed up the portable parts of St. George's, taking special care of the cross and plaque. We crated the organ and saw everything safely loaded onto lorries for the train journey. We were due to move out at 2.30am on Easter Day. The Church was packed at 11pm on Easter Eve when I celebrated Holy Communion for the last time in the mosque. The heavy furniture was to be moved to another area and stored.

Parties of 600 left Singapore Station each morning for the trip to Thailand. Herded into a lorry the 28 men in my party were decanted at the station into an iron goods truck which was to be our shelter for the next 5 days. It was a nightmare – the trucks were without springs and entirely built of iron. Five days and nights of rattling, bumping, shaking, in sweltering tropical heat and sweating human bodies proves that the human frame can stand up to real toughness. So we travelled the lengths of Malaya – a series of plantations interspersed with the densest jungle – parts awe-inspiring scenery, great rugged hills, tin mines, and later miles and miles of paddy fields. It was not possible to sleep at night as there was only room just to sit down, perhaps on a bag or pack, latrines there were not.

Food was erratic. Tubs of rice and sun dried, evil smelling fish would be a 24 hour ration, ½ a pint of hot water per man each day did little to quench parched throats. I was experiencing for about the first time the status of a prisoner of war and to me the cheerfulness of the men belied our true position. The train would stop usually in the middle of the night for an hour or 2 and if you were lucky you might find a spot of water for a wash. On one rare occasion we were allowed to buy bananas from hawkers on a station. At other times the Jap guards drove off our men at the point of a bayonet for any contact with the Malays.

At last we disembarked about 40 miles from Bangkok at the small town of Bampong. Here we were to realise how false were the promises of the I.J.A. A small town was Bampong, yet it was the base for administering to the 80,000 prisoners British, Australian and Dutch, as well as a base for operations in Burma. After an hour's wait in the main street we were marched carrying our kit to a base camp two miles away. Many collapsed under heavy loads. The camp consisted of several roughly built huts with atap roofs. Here we were herded and bullied and struck, tired and disappointed men. Food was a vegetable stew served 3 times daily – we have called it Jungle stew, and it consists of a small assortment of chopped vegs cooked in water with rice as an extra. In the evening issue a few pieces of tough fibrous substance enabled it to be called meat stew. All our kit except that which we could carry was stacked in heaps in the town. The following evening we learnt we had a 160 mile march before us and we must cover 16 miles each night carrying our kit. I wonder if you realise how hopeless we felt. Promises of transport from train to camp had been made, we were told that 1/3 of our number would be unfit men. Remember too that the other 2/3 had been living on starvation diet for a year, had not slept for 5 nights, and were to lose their few cherished possessions. The "F" Force commander who was going ahead by lorry took charge of my Holy Communion set and the plaque of St. George.

Thailand seemed to be a flat rather uncharted country and, compared with Malaya, squalid. The people had been kind to us in so far as they could be with gifts of fruit (bananas and oranges) and cigarettes. But our spirits suffered another knock in our preparations for the march. If we attempted escape we should be shot, there was a price on each of our heads and the Thais never failed to return an escaped prisoner to the Nips. He would be returned dead or, if alive he was shot. Half a dozen known to me have met this fate so far. Any men, we were told, who fell out of the march tho exhausted must not be left as Thais stripped the victim and were liable to knife him. Further up-country when the route was through jungle trails, we must be prepared for tigers, snakes and elephants. Such embarrassments though were regarded with amusement.

Our party of 600 paraded on the road outside this base camp at 10pm and stood around for an hour, whilst excitable, gesticulating guards dashed about checking and counting. Each man was loaded with all he could manage. We were able to sell oddments of kit to the Thais and so were in possession of several dollars. So we marched, resting ¼ of hour in each hour, with a halt at about 3 am. for a drink of hot water. Never have I enjoyed a rest so much. Equipment thrown aside, one could lie flat on the metalled road, the heat from the surface dried the sweat soaked clothes. Many men collapsed. When this happened the procedure was first to carry his kit and allow him to stagger, with the help of friends. If he passed right out then his kit was abandoned and he would be carried on a stretcher.

As dawn broke we neared our first destination and an amusing and kindly event occurred. Our Nip guards 1 in front and 2 in the rear hired rickshaws and then bounded past the tired column with those who had fallen out. The rickshaws were hired by the guards. The staging camp consisted of a piece of scrub land with a small shed for the use of the guards and that's all. We removed our boots, found some shade and slept. Awake at midday we discovered a Buddhist temple next to which was a small market housed in an open sided rather elaborate shed presumably used for meetings. Here could be bought fried eggs and numerous local dishes. This food was most attractive and tasty and a sweet black coffee became a favourite. Jungle stew was eventually supplied but few ate it. Many men had a few dollars by the selling of personal kit, watches, fountain pens, rings and the like. The weeks that followed our arrival would have been unbearably miserable without these sums of money.

With nightfall came rain, the monsoon is due in a month or two and again we scrambled through mud and puddles to the road. A small body of men had to be left under a lean-to shed in the care of one of the M.O.s. The trek began, muscles ached, blisters were painful and clinging wet shirts and shorts made one feel that the lot of the prisoner can be unbelievably miserable. I honestly believe that cattle handled as we were would result in prosecution for cruelty.

As dawn pierced the dull grey clouds we arrived at the next staging camp. Here we were to spend 36 hours, a night's rest would mean much. For me this camp 2 miles outside the ancient walled village of Kanchanaburi had special significance. A Hospital was formed under the now familiar furnished shed, 150 men were sprawled on the floor, 1500 men were camping in the bushes and scrub. It was here that the M.O., seeing blood on my shorts, ordered me to stay behind when he discovered that I was bleeding from haemorrhoids. This condition was brought on by the appalling train journey and was aggravated and indeed painful during the 34 mile march. To my regret I was forced to become a patient and with ½ a dozen others was ordered to a British Hospital in Kanchanaburi. The Nip soldiers inspected each person and laughed at our so called serious cases. He said a truck would come the next afternoon. It was 3 days later when we were admitted to Hospital.

It was a base hospital of 1000 and served the camps up-country. Here an operation soon put me on my feet and I was there 8 days and 11 times I was called to administer to dying men. The wards were atap huts with raised platforms but no beds or bedding, and these were crammed with dysentery, malaria, vitamin deficiency and eye patients as well as several 100s of surgical cases. I will not dwell on the horror of the dysentery wards. Living skeletons so many were. It was a great privilege to administer to those who needed you. It was a real thrill to meet again men, it must have been several hundred, who had been a part of St. George's. The daily services were enthusiastically supported. I noted that the hymn sheets produced in the Hospital were copies of the St. George's ones. The Dental Officer has been doing a grand job in running Sunday services. To read this may seem grim and morbid, but tho life is hard it is real and fine. I would tho mention the funerals.

A party marched out each day to Kanburi (as it is locally called) and 4 hours' work completed preparations. A plot of rough ground had been given by the Thais in one of their cemeteries. This doesn't mean the familiar English picture. Several temples bordered the plot, a tin shed formed one side and this was a so called crematorium. Next was a kind of grid with a corrugated iron roof making the open air cemeteries. The only evidence that this might be a burial ground is the presence of a dozen decorated cone shaped ornaments, each in need of repair, but I don't believe anything in this country is ever repaired. When a Thai is buried a hole is knocked in the plaster of one of these cones and the ashes of the deceased poured in. Our plot has been cleared and 80 graves with a cross on each gives evidence of our faith. One regrets the fact that cattle trample the area, and that occasional crosses disappear, probably as firewood, but no disrespect is intended. I always insist on the Thais and Nip guards taking part in the service. The latter are punctilious in their army etiquette.

After the ceremony was over and the grave filled, the burial party and guard and myself in white tho stained cassock and felt hat, went down to the river to swim. Our nakedness did not arouse the slightest attention from the many river loungers. The villagers would give us bananas and coffee and an amusing half hour would be spent petting the children and talking in signs to the parents. These funerals were unfortunately a daily event and entailed a 4 mile walk and the body had to be carried on a stretcher.

A pencil sketch by POW R J Gamble of the simple cemetery at Kanburi where many of the prisoners who had died working on the Burma Railway were buried.

KANBURI STAGING CAMP
June - August '43

In the middle of the night ten days after I had been admitted into this hospital I was ordered to board a truck and soon found myself back at the staging camp at Kanburi. Life in the scrubland settled down to a routine. No further parties arrived and the camp of 600 settled down to make the best of poor surroundings. We built little shacks from bamboo and sacks, using any oddment of equipment that had been jettisoned by the earlier parties. I found myself on what we termed the "staff", the only Englishman among 10 Australians. We shared a tent, there were several other tents and the big open-sided shed and a smaller one for the Nip guards. This camp was not fenced in and in theory we could wander anywhere, tho in practice the only sign of civilisation was the straight road to Burma which passed the camp and a few huts owned by the peasant people. It seemed that we were to be separated from the force of 2000 now scattered 100 miles away on this Burma road. Occasionally trucks would pull up at this camp and give us graphic details of conditions up-country. Rice and a few sweet potatoes provided the 2 meals a day. Sickness was decimating the numbers and cholera had broken out, 170 cases were reported in one camp. To us it did not seem possible for these men to live.

About a month passed and suddenly we were informed that all men who were fit would be sent up-country by lorry to join the main body of our force. Naturally we all wanted to go in this party as we wanted to join our main party. For those who still believed the Japanese promises we were assured of good camps in pleasant surroundings; needless to say, conditions were terrible. We were soon to learn the measure of power which was wielded by the ordinary Japanese soldier. Our "F" Force Guard (Shimizu) himself selected the party to go on and detailed those to remain, fitness or otherwise was not the deciding factor. Unhappily for me, he knew me and in his own way professed a liking for me, so to my dismay I was to remain behind with the 150 sick and the M.O. and interpreter. Our own desires were of no avail, we had no contact with the main force, no pressure could be brought to bear. I wrote and sent verbal messages by Japanese soldiers in an effort to contact our own commander. I was restless and unhappy, but did my best with the few under my care.

Our Nip guards were anxious to remain in our present camp and made life as tolerable as possible. The C.O. of the Camp, a doctor and I were sometimes invited to supper with our guards who were 2 young soldiers of peasant type. Seated tailor-fashion cross-legged on a wooden platform we enjoyed a superior meal of pork fried in batter. On one occasion they took us to an open air cinema in Kanburi to witness Jap propaganda films. We seemed to be the only British among 1000s of Japanese soldiers. Permission was given for me to organise a canteen buying our supplies from a nearby Thai police station. I never saw any evidence of its use as a police H.Q. It swarmed with a family of most attractive children, and here again an occasional meal supplemented our monotonous and meagre rations. With the Nips we made clumsy use of chopsticks. In any Thai meals fingers only were necessary and from a dozen little dishes tasty spiced pieces of food were eaten. The young mother of 6 squatted on a form, whilst she fed the baby and placed balls of rice in the mouths of the younger children. It was a queer house, a very superior product compared with the squalor of the peasants – but in spite of its two rooms downstairs and 3 up, all meals were eaten in a dirty yard, where chickens and flies and dogs added an air of confusion to the one of general untidiness.

We built an open air Altar which I used for celebrations, whilst the evening services were informal and took place in the open shed. They were held in the dark, and everyone attended, tho I told them they could clear out before I began: a talk, some prayers and a part of a hymn. I have said that my Church kit was up-country – so a chalice was made from a metal funnel plugged and fastened into a wooden base and a tin lid was the paten. At first I used dry biscuits and a local wine given by some friendly Thais, but later I was brought some real wafers and wine by a Christian Jap returning from a visit to Singapore. In describing the Church built here it compares poorly with the St. George's of Changi – but still, a grand little chapel has been created, built entirely from odds and ends found in the camp and the only tool is a 4 ½ " saw. The Chapel is built with bamboo uprights and grass mats form the sides and back, it is roofed with tarpaulin. The Altar is made from bamboo and mats with interlaced basket-like material as a reredos or background. Cross and candles are from bamboo as are the Altar rails. Marmite jars are the flower vases – it is really quite an impressive little shrine and much admired by our Nip guards – and used well by us all. Each evening at sun-down we wander across to say our evening prayers.

Pencil sketch of St George's Mark 11 in Kanburi close to the River Kwai. This "grand little chapel" was built entirely from odds and ends found round the camp. It had bamboo uprights, grass mats and was roofed with tarpaulin. *Sketched by a POW 1.9.43.*

For three months we have lived in Thailand, our little camp ticks over in a regular and ordered routine. We are still separated from our main party by 140 miles but expect to link up eventually. Stragglers came back here from the other hospitals. I understand that there are 12,000 casualties in camp hospitals within a few miles of our community. Conditions here have improved, we are now housed in a hut. This building is typical of the local homes of the people and is a miracle of construction. Twenty Thai workers with no other tools than a half crown handsaw built our hut which accommodates over 100 men, in less than a week, no nail or screw is used, simply lengths of bamboo tied together with rattan and roofed with atap. Platforms of split bamboo run the length of the hut and on these we live and sleep. The Church has been enlarged and continues to be well used, 2 classes for Confirmation have been completed and the little service of prayers each night is well attended. I mentioned casually to the Nip guard in command that my portable organ had been seen amongst the piles of kit dumped at Bampong. He is a queer little man and soon the crated organ arrived. After a day's pathetic wailing of some oriental melody, I have taught him to play Abide with Me – perhaps the first step in conversion from Buddhism, I'm afraid the old hymn tune is being massacred, still it is preferable to his previous efforts.

In common with the majority of our number I am suffering as Job of old did – not boils but a mass of skin eruptions, impetigo, tinea, tropical sores and ulcers. How perfectly foul and disgusting it is. This means miserable sleepless nights due to incessant itching – this condition is, I suppose, due to the dust and dirt around us, and the lack of water for washing and the very poor condition of our bodies.

Sartorially we are not so well equipped as this time last year. And the march too, here, has taken its toll. We all wear only a pair of patched shorts and wooden clogs, there are those whose shirts are finished and now wear a strip of cloth passed between the legs and fastened front and back with tape. In those who still have bits of clothes at bedtime the ordinary custom is reversed – here one gets dressed for bed – the air cools a little before the dawn. It is always tricky getting one's blanket (if one possesses one) laid out. There are 12 of us who sleep on a platform 12 feet by the same width, say about the same area as a small room in an English home. There is no light, and mosquito nets to be fixed. For some time now sleep has been so difficult to come by, perhaps it is the lack of physical exercise or one's active mind. For hours, sometimes till dawn, my mind races over events of the past and plans for the future.

The Nip guard one day invited me to accompany him to town to buy goods for our canteen. It was a tremendous thrill to visit the walled city of Kanburi and see again the busy life of an oriental city with crowded shops and stalls, the shrill tinkle of bicycle bells the hooting from motor vehicles – it seemed to me that I was surrounded by the rush and noise of Oxford Street. I was amused to watch the Jap soldier and Thai tradesman haggling over prices in atrocious pidgin English, neither knew each other's language, but a smattering of English seemed to be the common denominator. Our purchases included peanut toffee, cakes made from dates and pork fat and garlic, duck eggs at 10 cents each, cigs and tobacco (local brands), bananas at a cent each, flour, brown sugar and dried fish were among the items. This canteen is a great boon as we now send out working parties of our fit men, who sweat through the day shovelling gravel or such similar work, and who receive 10 cents pay a day. The coolies who form conscript labour and live nearby receive the princely sum of a dollar a day or in our money about a shilling. Surely we should be depressed and dejected? We, a surrendered force, the officers should have committed hari kari – yet we joke and laugh, confidently pulling the legs of the guards, assuring them that the fall of Nippon is not far off.

The large open-sided shed that housed so many when the troops were marching through up-country and pausing here for a night and under which so many of our present numbers lived, has now been fitted with desks and forms and the rest of the paraphernalia that go to make a village school. And here in our midst, a stone's throw from our hut is a Thai school with many dozens of small children attending daily for classes. No wire separates us from them.

Thailand is the land of Buddhism and every village has its colourful and attractive temples, the bigger villages rival our Welsh villages in their number of places of worship. Each has too, its little shrine and the folk are keen to observe at any rate the outward appearance of devotion. A usual sight for our camp is the wandering groups of monks each dressed alike in bright yellow robes with shaven heads protected by an open umbrella. Two amusing incidents concern these holy men. When we were resting after having marched some way from the station, a few passed murmuring "Parker Pen" – they knew a good fountain pen, and too, they knew we needed money. On the other occasion four or five solemnly shuffled past us and the leader, who seemed to be lost in oriental contemplation, raised one hand and made the victory "V" sign and muttered "OK".

KANBURI HOSPITAL CAMP
AUGUST '43 – APRIL '44

The last weeks in this small camp have been irksome. I have tried again and again to get permission to join the main force and do the work as Senior Chaplain but my pleas have had no effect on the Nip general – but at last in August after repeated requests I was suddenly transferred to a new Hospital which was to be formed a mile or so away and was to serve our force.

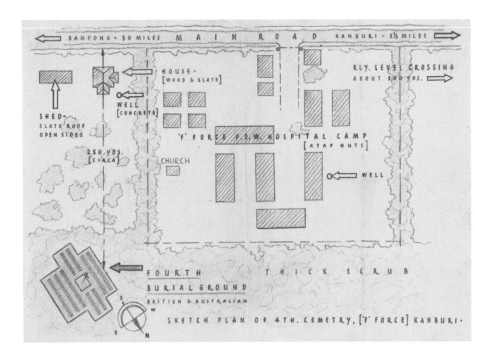

Detailed plan of the makeshift hospital and the site of the 4th Burial Ground in Kanburi used by 'F' Force. 45% of the men in 'F' Force died working on the Burma Railway.

It now appeared that the work of building a Railway into Burma had been completed, and gradually the force was to be withdrawn and would pass through this Hospital. The camp was situated between the main road to Burma and the Railway and no expansion was possible. Immediately on arrival I drew up orders for procedure in the case of seriously ill and dangerously ill patients and these cases were notified to me at once. In this way I was able to visit and pray with each man before he died, nearly always he died in my presence.

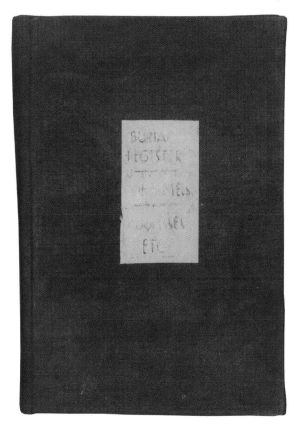

The battered cover of Eric's second Burial Register in which he kept details of every prisoner he buried. He recorded their name, rank and cause of death and the number and position of their grave.

It will be necessary to give some idea of the months the men spent on the Thai-Burma border in order to understand the appalling tragedy – events which would, I believe, stagger the world outside. The reason for these many parties up-country was to construct a railway line over a distance of 400 miles. A project which, for years, had been rejected by British Engineers, but the conquerors of Thailand thought differently. The line has been constructed, traffic proceeds from Thailand to Burma – but it has cost over 20,000 lives of prisoners. Close on half of my force of 7000 are dead, up to a dozen are dying now each day. Elaborate medical terms can describe the cause of death, cardiac beri beri , dysentery, malaria, but the root cause is sheer starvation.

A page from Eric's Burial Register in which he recorded the deaths of his fellow prisoners. He notes the precise time of death (0500 hours) of one man, 26 year old Frederick Stanbury, his Batman and the verger of his church in Changi who died of Beri-beri and heart failure after amoebic dysentery at 0500 on April 1st 1944. Presumably Eric was at his bedside when he died. Frederick's artistry with flowers, noted with admiration in Chapter 1, is reflected in the inscription on his gravestone at Kanburi War Cemetery, "One of God's loveliest flowers that ever bloomed".

In months these men have lived in dense jungle with no shelter during the rains, their food has been plain rice, often as little as 3 spoonsful 3 times a day, flavoured with onion and bean water. Men would be turned out before dawn, given a portion of rice and marched perhaps a mile or two to the railway. Here cuttings and embankments were being made. Bridges built, routes blasted through rock forms. Work would cease with the coming of darkness and they would be marched back to camp. Rain continued for days at a time. Men collapsed with malaria, dysentery, tropical ulcers, huge open wounds as large as a plate, many amputations followed these ulcers. Side by side with the prisoners worked conscripted coolie labour and (from them) soon swept through an epidemic of cholera, decimating our forces.

The men were worn out by work which had kept them slaving during the hours of daylight, in almost continuous rain, barefooted because boots had fallen to pieces during the march, with no clothes except a ragged pair of shorts or some sort of rag for a loin cloth. Men were stunned and apathetic, but slowly the spiritual side revived and flourished as never before. Men had been so near death – life for them had been stripped of its veneer, stark reality had faced them, they expected to be met on those terms. They talked about death and many is the time at the bedside of a dying man he has asked me to pray for his death, for his peace, for release from his abject misery.

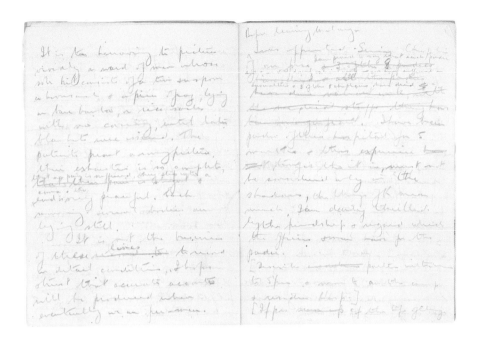

A page from Eric's notes, written hastily and in secret into a Thai child's exercise book.
"It is too harrowing to picture vividly a ward of men whose sole kit consists of a tin
and a spoon, a haversack and a piece of rag, lying on bare bamboo."

As I write now in this makeshift hospital I wonder what will be the outcome. In the past several months I have buried over 600 men. The hospital has 3000 patients, more and more come from up-country as room becomes available. It is just time to say that of the 7000 there are perhaps 1000 reasonably fit. The rest have died or are in hospital. It is too harrowing to picture vividly a ward of men whose sole kit consists of a tin and a spoon and a haversack and a piece of rag, lying on bare bamboo, or rice sacks with no covering, until later blankets were issued. The patients present a sorry picture, their exhaustion is so complete that no pain is suffered, they slip into a coma and the end is peaceful. Each morning several bodies are lying still. It is not the business of these lines to record conditions in detail. I hope and trust that accurate accounts will be produced when eventually we are free men.

Late in November and through December, first the fit and later the sick were moved from Thailand back to Singapore. Eight hundred of the most serious cases of "F" and "H" Forces were to be left for three months. I decided that my responsibility was to remain with those very sick men. These months before Christmas '43 were so completely different from the previous year. I am reminded of the mud and maggots – the paddyfield on which our 30 hut hospital stood had a path running the length of the camp, huts stood close together on either side of the track – in consequence it was thick dust or liquid mud. The maggots are not fiction. At the opposite ends of the huts away from this path were our latrines - large open trenches from which millions of large maggots were seething and forever attempting to crawl away from these pits. How could this compare with the ordered life of Changi?

I have been padre of this hospital for 5 months and this experience, tragic though it is, must not be considered only in the shadows, the things of Christianity mean much, I am daily thrilled by the friendship and regard which the officers and men have for the padre.

The next four months (Jan. to Apr., 1944) were happy and I believe profitable months. My church kit had been brought from store at Bampong, the Communion Set and St. George's Plaque which it had been necessary to abandon in a jungle-staging camp turned up a little the worse for rain and sun. I rescued my Chalice and Paten from some Jap guard rooms where they had been used as ash trays. So it was that at Christmas an Altar was put up using the same furnishings as used at St. George's a year ago. Communicants over Christmas amounted to 200 of our strength of 800. Men were coming through the daze of the past months, health was coming back to body, mind and spirits.

After a few weeks the bed-down patients were reduced to about 50% and they were becoming bored with no books or the means of entertainment. For ten weeks and four evenings a week I attempted in talks in an intended humorous vein, a series of descriptions of Life in the slums and Cotswolds – this seemed to fill a gap and was appreciated in a way that amazed me.

On April 24, 1944, camp having been dismantled, we entrained and after a tedious journey arrived at Singapore on the 29th. My year's work in Thailand was over. To me a year, the toughest of my life, grim and shocking as it was, yet on reflection a year I would not have missed; I have learnt much – but a year I would never wish to live through again. Eight Chaplains were in this Force, three are buried in Thailand.

* * * *

In these accounts, Eric Cordingly left out what may have been his most frightening experience on the Burma Railway - an episode in which he was beaten and thrown into a pit. Many years later, he told this story at a school prize-giving in Norfolk. The headmaster asked him to write it down and, in a letter to the school in 1975, this is what he wrote:

From a jungle camp near the River Kwai in Thailand, prisoners-of-war who had survived work on the railway and were living in a hutted camp, were allowed by the Japanese guards to go to the river for washing and swimming. It was something all those who were fit enough enjoyed doing, especially since we were sometimes able to meet prisoners from other camps and were thus able to get news of friends.

I went with this party whenever possible and since most men had no clothes but a tattered loin cloth and I still possessed a pair of shorts and was in charge of the party, I had been given notes scribbled by men asking for news of friends. These notes I would hand to the senior prisoners of other parties whom we might meet.

As we passed the guard hut we were, on this occasion, stopped and searched, and I was found with these written notes, as was an Indian doctor in the party. He and I were taken to the Guard commander and accused of being spies. The doctor and I were then hand-cuffed to each other and taken to a pit outside the guard hut (the pit was a deep air raid pit for the use of the guards and was about 10/12 feet deep and about 4 feet square). We were placed in this pit and left handcuffed until it was decided what action should be taken.

In the early hours of the morning before it was light a bamboo ladder was lowered into the pit and down it came a young Japanese soldier, presumably the guard on duty. He had with him a container of sweetened tea and two bananas. His knowledge of English was as slight as ours of Japanese. He indicated that he was a Christian and he knew that I was a Christian priest. Trembling and fearful he told us to eat and drink quickly and in a few moments he was gone.

Many hours later we were taken from the pit and told that we were to be allowed to re-join the prisoners in the camp. I did not see the Japanese soldier again who had visited us and would in fact not have recognised him, but I know that if he had been discovered by the Guard commander he would have been summarily executed for the action he took in caring for enemy prisoners.

Throughout our years of captivity we came across very few Japanese Christians and I shall always remember this young Japanese soldier who wonderfully demonstrated his faith.

Under the Shadow of the Gaol Walls
April 1944 – September 1945
Changi Prison, Singapore
Eric Cordingly's military report

On my return to Singapore from Thailand, I spent a few weeks in the Hospital Area, and during this time the Camp was moved into Changi Gaol and huts around the walls of the prison were built to house the 12000 prisoners of war. Over 5000 were living in the Gaol, which was built to cope with 800 Asiatics.

Within a week or so of arrival in this camp permission was given to build a standard type of Church. A simple shelter 14 feet by 10 feet, which was simply the Chancel and a cover for the Altar, the rest of the Church was open air. I was put in charge of a working group of 2500, and soon St. George's Church, Mark iii was built. Mark ii was my Church in Kanburi, Thailand. In a very short while flowers and creepers hid the structure, and with flower beds the site was most attractive. Plaited palm fronds formed the outside walls of the Nave. Permanent benches were fixed to seat two hundred, extra forms were brought in for Sunday services. This third edition of St. George's was still fitted with its characteristic furnishings described earlier.

St George's Mark III June 44 – March 45 was constructed in No 2 Working Camp, which was situated immediately to the south and outside the Gaol building itself, but within Changi's prison walls. It was furnished with the plaque, the brass cross, the pulpit and other pieces from the first St George's. *Water colour painting by Lieut. E Stacy R.E.*

The next six months was a busy time, and a hard one. Though the war news was good, men were in a difficult mood – we could not see the end of hostilities in East Asia. Work on the air strip was extremely arduous and long, rations were at starvation level. Until the surrender our rations consisted of about eight ounzes of rice a day, a little crude palm oil, salt, tea, and sometimes an ounze or two of dried fish – this was our entire ration, except for coarse green leaf vegetables which we grew ourselves. Most people lost from three to seven stone, and the average weight could not have been much over eight stone – each month three or four pounds weight would be lost. Men looked gaunt and haggard. To me it is an amazing thing that they managed to march the four miles to the aerodrome and then work throughout the heat of the day as labourers.

Men came to church on Sundays in great numbers, but they were, I think, too tired for much during the week, though the daily Celebrations and evening prayers were always attended by a few.

This sphere of work was suddenly stopped when the I.J.A. closed the area and sent the men to working parties in the town. I was then placed in charge of the Officers' Area by the A/A.C.G. early in this year. This had 1200 officers, 300 of whom were Dutch.

This was thrilling work, and I think in many ways my happiest. A volunteer party of fifty officers moved the Church from the old site to the new, and in 24 hours we had the complete Church on its new site, complete with its seating – this was St. George's Mark.IV.

St George's Mk IV April – September 45. St George's Mk III had been moved to the Officers' Area of Changi prison. It was surrounded by their poultry runs so it was affectionately known as St Georges-in-the-Poultry. *Water colour painting by Lieut. E. Stacy*

A selection of colourful Christmas cards Eric received from fellow captives for Christmas 1944.

Birthday card sent to Eric by fellow prisoners Eddie and Eric May 1945.

Things flourished in this area, and the response was truly amazing. Regular Evensong was packed with 400-500 officers, assisted by an excellent choir of twenty, trained by the organist of Singapore Cathedral (a Lieut.Col). The daily Celebration of Holy Communion averaged about ten, and Sundays numbered about 150. Daily Compline brought its regular numbers, especially from the "embryo" Ordinands.

Refresher courses for Confirmation continued three afternoons each week throughout this period, and it was to me a fine thing that in a class of thirty, half a dozen Lt. Colonels would be among this group of officers. Over 450 have been through this fourteen-talk preparation. As news from the outside world became exciting, officers began flocking to my quarter in order to "straighten things out" as they put it. Ordination classes, too, were continued through this time.

A grand post-script may be added when, after the I.J.A. surrender, on September 7th, the Bishop of Singapore again visited the camp, and confirmed 120 who had been prepared. (During our captivity the Bishop has suffered ill-treatment and torture at the hands of the Jap secret police).

A photograph of the Confirmation Service at which Bishop Leonard Wilson officiated on September 7th 1945 in St Paul's Church in Changi Gaol, which later appeared in the Illustrated London News. The POWs are wearing newly issued clothing, the first they had received for many months. Eric's head can be seen below the lamp on the right hand side of the altar. His wife, Mary, saw the photograph in a shop window in Cheltenham and realised that he had survived.

In conclusion, I must express my gratitude for the real help and kindness I have received from the A/A.C.G., and for the friendliness and co-operation of my brother Chaplains. Each Monday morning we had a Staff meeting attended by all Chaplains (except R.C.). There were two other Anglican Churches (one in the Gaol, and another in the Hospital Area), as well as one Church of Scotland, and one R.C. Church. At this Monday meeting A.I.F., and Dutch Protestant Chaplains attended as well as ourselves. Each Thursday morning for the past year all C. of E. Chaplains met for a Discussion Group.

In summing up I would say that as a parish priest the past three and a half years has been the most wonderful in my life, in spite of the grim and hungry times. We might have been prohibited from working, but the reverse was true. (I believe the Japs to be very superstitious, I found this time after time, and they were rather afraid to ban religion. They stopped all other meetings, entertainments and social gatherings, but never interfered with our Church activities.)

I am most grateful for this chance we have had, which, I believe will affect in some real measure the lives of many thousands of men, who have come to grips with the Church under the various padres for the first time in their lives.

E.W.B CORDINGLY, C.F.

A.C.G.s Office,

Twelfth Army Headquarters

RANGOON

September 11 1945

Epilogue: 'Purpose in Living'
1945 - 1976

"We were shattered at the end when parachuters came into the camp, and the brutal way they dealt with our captors," Eric Cordingly recalled in an interview with Anglia TV in 1974, "We had learned to live with them, we had got a way of life, we had got a faith, goodness mattered, caring for each other mattered, and this was something which meant a very great deal to us."

After their liberation, the prisoners remained in Changi for a short time. On 7th September 1945 the Bishop of Singapore returned to the liberated Changi Prison to hold a confirmation service. A picture of this service was published in the Illustrated London News. In Cheltenham, Eric's wife, Mary, saw this photograph displayed in a shop window and immediately recognised her husband standing under a lamp at the altar of the small chapel. It was proof that he had survived. "I couldn't feel my legs as I walked home," she told her family years later, "I know what it means to say you are walking on air."

Eric Cordingly arrived in the UK on 13th October 1945. He had been away from home for four years.

"I do not wish to dwell on the horror of prison life," he told the Gloucestershire Echo, "No doubt in the months to come the full story will be given and become known to the world [...] I think it is undesirable at the present moment for these stories to get around, as exaggerated reports have already caused considerable distress."

"There used to be a flat-topped wall on either side of the iron gates to the Rectory," remembers David Cordingly, "Standing on the wall provided a grandstand view of the German prisoner-of-war camp in the field opposite as well as a view across the churchyard to any weddings or funerals that might be taking place. On the day of Daddy's return John and I spent much of the morning on the wall. Someone had hung lots of flags and bunting across the gate and I think there was a 'Welcome Home' banner as well. This meant that everyone passing along the lane asked us when our father was expected.

"I don't remember the drive to the station or who was in the car with us and I don't remember being curious or excited at the thought of seeing one's father after an absence of four years or so. I had no idea what he would look like. I do remember the first sight of a gaunt figure with glasses in a khaki uniform, and I remember the triumphal journey back through the village with several stops en route to greet people. I vaguely remember the photographer from the Gloucestershire Echo gathering us together for that photograph.

A picture taken minutes after his arrival home shows Eric standing next to Mary
and holding 6 year old David's hand. 4 year old John is standing in front of
Mary's grandmother, Josephine Smith. The taxi is still in the background.

"The big disappointment was the present which he brought back. Presents
seemed very important in those days when there were hardly any toys around.
He'd managed to purchase two wooden scooters on his voyage home. The
problem was that the scooters' small wooden wheels were useless on the gravel
drive and there was nowhere smooth enough to get them going properly. I have
no recollection of the rest of the day or indeed of the days that followed. I do
know that Daddy more than made up for the disappointment of the scooters
by the amount of time he devoted to making things for us: building cranes in
Meccano, constructing an amazingly elaborate train layout for the Hornby
Dublo trains, and later a puppet theatre and a Heron dinghy."

In the months after his return, Cordingly spent many hours in his study writing to the families of those prisoners he'd cared for before they died. It took time for him to recover his physical strength; in later years he suffered recurring bouts of dengue fever. But he and Mary were able to resume life with their family. In 1946 they had a daughter, Louise. Their youngest son, Christopher, was born in 1953.

Eric Cordingly went on to serve as Rector of Stevenage, Chaplain to the Queen, Residentiary Canon of Norwich Cathedral and Archdeacon of Norfolk. In 1963, he was consecrated Bishop of Thetford. He died of cancer in 1976 at the age of 65. His widow, Mary, died in 2011. Their ashes are buried in the Jesus Chapel of Norwich Cathedral.

Two decades after he was released, Eric Cordingly reflected on his years in captivity in a collection of prisoners' experiences, published as *Beyond Hatred*.

Beyond Hatred, Eric Cordingly, 1967

There is no doubt that those three and a half years were a wonderful opportunity for a parish priest, and I suppose in fact the most wonderful time in my life, in spite of the grim and hungry times. We might have been prohibited from working but the reverse was true. The Japanese stopped all other meetings at various times, together with entertainments and social gatherings, but they hardly ever interfered with our church activities. One had an opportunity as a priest of doing something which is denied to us in our ordinary life here at home. For once, and for three and a half years, the thin veneer of civilization, or reticence, had been stripped from men. We were all down to bedrock. One saw people as they really were. There was no reason for humbug or cant; many men had no use at all for religion, but great numbers had – and these men were no longer shy about the faith which they had found.

I miss the comradeship and the ease of discussion and talk. I resent the barriers which are now once again firmly erected between those who believe and those who don't, between those who are ordained and those who are not. I have referred to the fact that these years were, from my point of view, good years. There was no sense of frustration in one's job as a parish priest. One built on the simple fundamental faith. Life was basic and so was faith. Rules and regulations seemed, and were, unimportant. We were not bound by the legalities of orthodox religion. There was no compulsion about churchgoing, nor was it undertaken because of tradition or custom; it was our need. There was a gaiety and simple joy which was shared by all those who were part of this fellowship.

And what has all this meant? This experience is now more than twenty five years old. Has it any bearing on the lives which are ours today? I often wonder. Looking back to the really grim time in the jungle camp beside the Railway, the truly remarkable thing was the way the human spirit rose to magnificent heights. After months of sheer degradation, gradually the spirit to care for each other revived, incredible kindness and self-sacrifice was in evidence.

Within the camp were men of all sorts, officers, other ranks, local volunteer forces recruited in Malaya, regular soldiers, professional men, business executives, and the strange thing was that seemingly ordinary men, of no particular calibre or character, often stood out head and shoulders above their fellows. Under the strain of this prison camp life only one thing prevailed and that was strength of character. Cleverness, learning, social background – these things didn't matter – only real goodness made any impact.

I remember so well the strangeness of the end of our captivity – the arrival of paratroopers from outside. In a sense, they were real outsiders. Perhaps this was due to our feeling that the life of the camp was the real life: the life which bore witness to what really counted in humanity – the spirit.

I suppose that some things stand out in greater contrast. One of the things which died in the prison camp was hate; I believe that we were all upset by the seemingly brutal way our captors were treated by those who relieved us at the end of our captivity. We had lost during those years the feeling to hate the Japanese, and, speaking personally, one of the things which hurts me more than anything is to read, even today, of man's inhumanity to man – of the incredible cruelty and indignity which man seems to inflict on his own kind.

And then, I think, I am really grateful for the things of this world, for the ordinary, material things, for food and for freedom. A most frequent nightmare, and this does not diminish, is the feeling of being a prisoner, of the loss of freedom, of the uncertainty of the future. Freedom is something we take for granted, it is simply part of our life. The loss of freedom is a terrible thing. As Christians we often pray, and perhaps with little real understanding, for justice and freedom; the human spirit must be free.

And then, as a parson, I have less tolerance for bigotry; I am inclined to think that rules and regulations don't matter much – it is the spirit that counts. If only one could strip down one's faith to the bare essentials, what a tremendous difference it would make! This is something we could all do together, but I realize we can't do it again today. We have built up our barriers, we have got back our reserve, we have put ourselves into categories, and this is a loss.

In the past twenty-five years, I have been frustrated so much by those things which are inhibiting the work of the Churches. In the prison camps we had perhaps returned to the simple faith and practice of the Acts of the Apostles, and this was good. I think I have still something of the vision of what might be, if only we could be stripped of those things which we regard as essential and yet are of no lasting worth. I do not simply mean the established forms and ceremonies and legal processes of my Church, though these need revision and pruning, but I mean the acceptance by ordinary people of so much that dims the light of faith – church services which are uninspiring and unreal, bad hymns, dismal chanting, I know that the services we shared in together were utterly real and sincere, and I suppose it was because we were for a while utterly real and sincere.

It is a strange thing how wonderful human beings are in adversity. I say this, having witnessed two dramatic defeats of arms. I know nothing of the glories of war, but only of its seamy side. There are aspects of Dunkirk and Singapore which make me feel a little ashamed, but the sheer adversity and grimness of three and a half years of prisoner-or-war life have made me feel proud to have shared a little of this experience. Basically, human nature is fine, and yet it seems that only in times of material prosperity do we lose a sense of our vision and purpose in living.

ACKNOWLEDGEMENTS

With huge thanks to my three brothers David, John and Christopher for their collaborative help and enormous support for this project. Special thanks to my husband Paul Reynolds, not only for his steadfast support, but also for his earlier research into my father's life and for his role in discovering the photographs of Eric in St George's Mark 1. I am enormously grateful to my son James who worked tirelessly with me to edit the papers and to my daughter Alice for her creative input and encouragement.

Special thanks also to Bernard Stogden for the use of his father's photograph of Eric, the story of which will be told in The Changi Cross. Also thanks to Bertie Boyce, ex POW, for his vivid memories of my father and St George's Mark 1.

My father wrote a chapter about his wartime experiences in *Beyond Hatred* edited by Guthrie Moir and published by Lutterworth Press in 1969. They have kindly allowed us to reprint extracts of his chapter in this book.

Permission has also been granted for use of the following photographs:

Confirmation Service 7th September 1945: Illustrated London News, Mary Evans Picture Library.

Homecoming photograph 13th October 1945 Gloucester Echo

Eric Cordingly's collection of papers includes a large number of original illustrations made by his fellow prisoners. We have included many of their sketches in this book. We are indebted to them for their work.

Thanks to Peter and Lucy at www.made-agency.co.uk

This book was typeset using 11pt Bell MT